Great Military Commanders

Douglas MacArthur

A Biography

Compiled by

Janina Milne

Scribbles

Year of Publication 2018

ISBN : 9789352979455

Book Published by

Scribbles

(An Imprint of Alpha Editions)

email - alphaedis@gmail.com

Produced by: PediaPress GmbH
Limburg an der Lahn
Germany
http://pediapress.com/

The content within this book was generated collaboratively by volunteers. Please be advised that nothing found here has necessarily been reviewed by people with the expertise required to provide you with complete, accurate or reliable information. Some information in this book may be misleading or simply wrong. Alpha Editions and PediaPress does not guarantee the validity of the information found here. If you need specific advice (for example, medical, legal, financial, or risk management) please seek a professional who is licensed or knowledgeable in that area.

Sources, licenses and contributors of the articles and images are listed in the section entitled "References". Parts of the books may be licensed under the GNU Free Documentation License. A copy of this license is included in the section entitled "GNU Free Documentation License"

The views and characters expressed in the book are those of the contributors and his/her imagination and do not represent the views of the Publisher.

Contents

Douglas MacArthur

<indicator name=”pp-default”> </indicator> <indicator name=”featured-star”> </indicator>

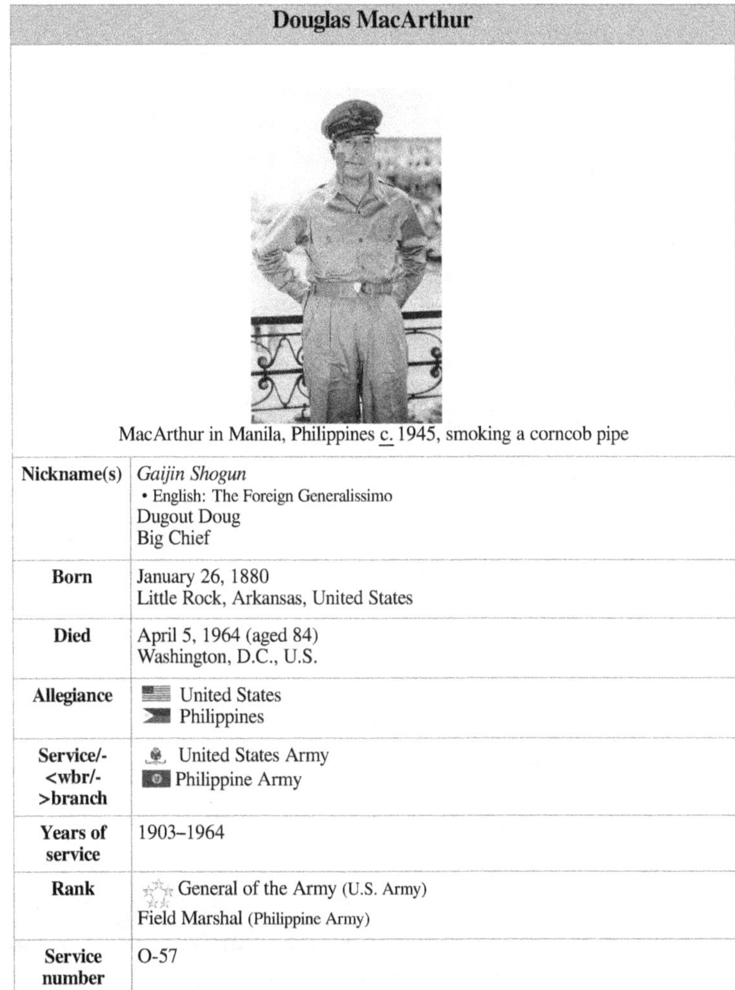

MacArthur in Manila, Philippines c. 1945, smoking a corncob pipe

Douglas MacArthur	
Nickname(s)	*Gaijin Shogun* • English: The Foreign Generalissimo Dugout Doug Big Chief
Born	January 26, 1880 Little Rock, Arkansas, United States
Died	April 5, 1964 (aged 84) Washington, D.C., U.S.
Allegiance	United States Philippines
Service/-<wbr/->branch	United States Army Philippine Army
Years of service	1903–1964
Rank	General of the Army (U.S. Army) Field Marshal (Philippine Army)
Service number	O-57

Commands held	United Nations Command Supreme Commander for the Allied Powers Southwest Pacific Area U.S. Army Forces Far East Philippine Department U.S. Army Chief of Staff Philippine Division U.S. Military Academy Superintendent 42nd Division 84th Infantry Brigade
Battles/wars	Mexican Revolution • United States occupation of Veracruz World War I • Champagne-Marne Offensive • Battle of Saint-Mihiel • Meuse-Argonne Offensive World War II • Philippines Campaign (1941–1942) • New Guinea campaign • Philippines Campaign (1944–1945) • Borneo campaign (1945) • Occupation of Japan Korean War • Battle of Inchon • UN Offensive, 1950 • Chinese Winter Offensive • UN Offensive, 1951
Awards	Medal of Honor Distinguished Service Cross (3) Army Distinguished Service Medal (5) Navy Distinguished Service Medal Silver Star (7) Distinguished Flying Cross Bronze Star Air Medal Purple Heart (2) *Complete list*
Spouse(s)	Louise Cromwell Brooks (m. 1922; divorce 1929) Jean Faircloth (m. 1937; his death 1964)
Children	Arthur MacArthur IV
Relations	*See MacArthur family*
Other work	Chairman of the board of Remington Rand
Signature	

Douglas MacArthur (26 January 1880 – 5 April 1964) was an American five-star general and Field Marshal of the Philippine Army. He was Chief of Staff of the United States Army during the 1930s and played a prominent role in the Pacific theater during World War II. He received the Medal of Honor for his service in the Philippines Campaign, which made him and his father Arthur MacArthur Jr., the first father and son to be awarded the medal. He was one of only five men ever to rise to the rank of General of the Army in the US Army, and the only man ever to become a field marshal in the Philippine Army.

Raised in a military family in the American Old West, MacArthur was valedictorian at the West Texas Military Academy, and First Captain at the United States Military Academy at West Point, where he graduated top of the class of 1903. During the 1914 United States occupation of Veracruz, he conducted a reconnaissance mission, for which he was nominated for the Medal of Honor. In 1917, he was promoted from major to colonel and became chief of staff of the 42nd (Rainbow) Division. In the fighting on the Western Front during World War I, he rose to the rank of brigadier general, was again nominated for a Medal of Honor, and was awarded the Distinguished Service Cross twice and the Silver Star seven times.

From 1919 to 1922, MacArthur served as Superintendent of the U.S. Military Academy at West Point, where he attempted a series of reforms. His next assignment was in the Philippines, where in 1924 he was instrumental in quelling the Philippine Scout Mutiny. In 1925, he became the Army's youngest major general. He served on the court martial of Brigadier General Billy Mitchell and was president of the American Olympic Committee during the 1928 Summer Olympics in Amsterdam. In 1930, he became Chief of Staff of the United States Army. As such, he was involved in the expulsion of the Bonus Army protesters from Washington, D.C. in 1932, and the establishment and organization of the Civilian Conservation Corps. He retired from the US Army in 1937 to become Military Advisor to the Commonwealth Government of the Philippines.

MacArthur was recalled to active duty in 1941 as commander of United States Army Forces in the Far East. A series of disasters followed, starting with the destruction of his air forces on 8 December 1941, and the invasion of the Philippines by the Japanese. MacArthur's forces were soon compelled to withdraw to Bataan, where they held out until May 1942. In March 1942, MacArthur, his family and his staff left nearby Corregidor Island in PT boats and escaped to Australia, where MacArthur became Supreme Commander, Southwest Pacific Area. Upon his arrival in Australia, MacArthur gave a speech in which he famously promised "I shall return" to the Philippines. After more than two years of fighting in the Pacific, he fulfilled that promise. For his defense of the Philippines, MacArthur was awarded the Medal of Honor. He officially accepted Japan's surrender on 2 September 1945, aboard USS *Missouri* anchored in Tokyo Bay, and oversaw the occupation of Japan from 1945 to 1951. As the effective ruler of Japan, he oversaw sweeping economic, political and social changes. He led the United Nations Command in the Korean War with initial success, however the controversial invasion of North Korea provoked Chinese intervention. Following a series of major defeats he was removed from command by President Harry S. Truman on 11 April 1951. He later became chairman of the board of Remington Rand.

Figure 1: *Douglas MacArthur as a student at West Texas Military Academy in the late 1890s*

Early life and education

A military brat, Douglas MacArthur was born 26 January 1880, at Little Rock Barracks, Little Rock, Arkansas, to Arthur MacArthur, Jr., a U.S. Army captain, and his wife, Mary Pinkney Hardy MacArthur (nicknamed "Pinky").[1] Arthur, Jr. was the son of Scottish-born jurist and politician Arthur MacArthur, Sr.,[2] Arthur would later receive the Medal of Honor for his actions with the Union Army in the Battle of Missionary Ridge during the American Civil War, and be promoted to the rank of lieutenant general.[3] Pinkney came from a prominent Norfolk, Virginia, family.[1] Two of her brothers had fought for the South in the Civil War, and refused to attend her wedding.[4] Arthur and Pinky had three sons, of whom Douglas was the youngest, following Arthur III, born on 1 August 1876, and Malcolm, born on 17 October 1878.[5] The family lived on a succession of Army posts in the American Old West. Conditions were primitive, and Malcolm died of measles in 1883.[6] In his memoir, *Reminiscences*, MacArthur wrote "I learned to ride and shoot even before I could read or write—indeed, almost before I could walk and talk."[7]

This time on the frontier ended in July 1889 when the family moved to Washington, D.C.,[8] where Douglas attended the Force Public School. His father was posted to San Antonio, Texas, in September 1893. While there MacArthur attended the West Texas Military Academy,[9] where he was awarded the gold medal for "scholarship and deportment". He also participated on the school tennis team, and played quarterback on the school football team and shortstop on its baseball team. He was named valedictorian, with a final year average of 97.33 out of 100.[10] MacArthur's father and grandfather unsuccessfully sought to secure Douglas a presidential appointment to the United States Military Academy at West Point, first from President Grover Cleveland and then from President William McKinley.[11] After these two rejections, he was given coaching and private tutoring by Milwaukee high school teacher Gertrude Hull. He then passed the examination for an appointment from Congressman Theobald Otjen,[9] scoring 93.3 on the test.[12] He later wrote: "It was a lesson I never forgot. Preparedness is the key to success and victory."[12]

MacArthur entered West Point on 13 June 1899,[13] and his mother also moved there to a suite at Craney's Hotel, overlooking the grounds of the Academy. Hazing was widespread at West Point at this time, and MacArthur and his classmate Ulysses S. Grant III were singled out for special attention by southern cadets as sons of generals with mothers living at Craney's. When Cadet Oscar Booz left West Point after being hazed and subsequently died of tuberculosis, there was a congressional inquiry. MacArthur was called to appear before a special Congressional committee in 1901, where he testified against cadets implicated in hazing, but downplayed his own hazing even though the other cadets gave the full story to the committee. Congress subsequently outlawed acts "of a harassing, tyrannical, abusive, shameful, insulting or humiliating nature", although hazing continued.[14] MacArthur was a corporal in Company B in his second year, a first sergeant in Company A in his third year and First Captain in his final year.[15] He played left field for the baseball team, and academically earned 2424.12 merits out of a possible 2470.00 or 98.14, the third highest score ever recorded, graduating first in his 93-man class on 11 June 1903.[16] At the time it was customary for the top-ranking cadets to be commissioned into the United States Army Corps of Engineers, so MacArthur was commissioned as a second lieutenant in that corps.[17]

Junior officer

MacArthur spent his graduation furlough with his parents at Fort Mason, California, where his father, now a major general, was serving as commander of the Department of the Pacific. Afterward, he joined the 3rd Engineer Battalion, which departed for the Philippines in October 1903. MacArthur was sent to Iloilo, where he supervised the construction of a wharf at Camp Jossman. He went on to conduct surveys at Tacloban City, Calbayog City and Cebu City. In November 1903, while working on Guimaras, he was ambushed by a pair of Filipino brigands or guerrillas; he shot and killed both with his pistol.[18] He was promoted to first lieutenant in Manila in April 1904.[19] In October 1904, his tour of duty was cut short when he contracted malaria and dhobi itch during a survey on Bataan. He returned to San Francisco, where he was assigned to the California Debris Commission. In July 1905, he became chief engineer of the Division of the Pacific.[20]

In October 1905, MacArthur received orders to proceed to Tokyo for appointment as aide-de-camp to his father. A man who knew the MacArthurs at this time wrote that: "Arthur MacArthur was the most flamboyantly egotistical man I had ever seen, until I met his son." They inspected Japanese military bases at Nagasaki, Kobe and Kyoto, then headed to India via Shanghai, Hong Kong, Java and Singapore, reaching Calcutta in January 1906. In India, they visited Madras, Tuticorin, Quetta, Karachi, the Northwest Frontier and the Khyber Pass. They then sailed to China via Bangkok and Saigon, and toured Canton, Tsingtao, Peking, Tientsin, Hankow and Shanghai before returning to Japan in June. The next month they returned to the United States,[21] where Arthur MacArthur resumed his duties at Fort Mason, still with Douglas as his aide. In September, Douglas received orders to report to the 2nd Engineer Battalion at the Washington Barracks and enroll in the Engineer School. While there he also served as "an aide to assist at White House functions" at the request of President Theodore Roosevelt.[22]

In August 1907, MacArthur was sent to the engineer district office in Milwaukee, where his parents were living. In April 1908, he was posted to Fort Leavenworth, where he was given his first command, Company K, 3rd Engineer Battalion.[22] He became battalion adjutant in 1909 and then engineer officer at Fort Leavenworth in 1910. MacArthur was promoted to captain in February 1911 and was appointed as head of the Military Engineering Department and the Field Engineer School. He participated in exercises at San Antonio, Texas, with the Maneuver Division in 1911 and served in Panama on detached duty in January and February 1912. The sudden death of their father on 5 September 1912 brought Douglas and his brother Arthur back to Milwaukee to care for their mother, whose health had deteriorated. MacArthur requested a transfer to Washington, D.C. so his mother could be near Johns Hopkins Hospital. Army Chief of Staff, Major General Leonard Wood, took up the matter with Secretary of War Henry L. Stimson, who arranged for MacArthur to be posted to the Office of the Chief of Staff in 1912.[23]

Veracruz expedition

On 21 April 1914, President Woodrow Wilson ordered the occupation of Veracruz. MacArthur joined the headquarters staff that was sent to the area, arriving on 1 May 1914. He realized that the logistic support of an advance from Veracruz would require the use of the railroad. Finding plenty of railroad cars in Veracruz but no locomotives, MacArthur set out to verify a report that there were a number of locomotives in Alvarado, Veracruz. For $150 in gold, he acquired a handcar and the services of three Mexicans, whom he disarmed. MacArthur and his party located five engines in Alvarado, two of which were only switchers, but the other three locomotives were exactly what was required. On the way back to Veracruz, his party was set upon by five armed men. The party made a run for it and outdistanced all but two of the armed men, whom MacArthur shot. Soon after, they were attacked by a group of about fifteen horsemen. MacArthur took three bullet holes in his clothes but was unharmed. One of his companions was lightly wounded before the horsemen finally decided to retire after MacArthur shot four of them. Further on, the party was attacked a third time by three mounted men. MacArthur received another bullet hole in his shirt, but his men, using their handcar, managed to outrun all but one of their attackers. MacArthur shot both that man and his horse, and the party had to remove the horse's carcass from the track before proceeding.[24]

A fellow officer wrote to Wood recommending that MacArthur's name be put forward for the Medal of Honor. Wood did so, and Chief of Staff Hugh L. Scott convened a board to consider the award.[25] The board questioned "the advisability of this enterprise having been undertaken without the knowledge of the commanding general on the ground".[26] This was Brigadier General Frederick Funston, a Medal of Honor recipient himself, who considered awarding the medal to MacArthur "entirely appropriate and justifiable".[27] However the board feared that "to bestow the award recommended might encourage any other staff officer, under similar conditions, to ignore the local commander, possibly interfering with the latter's plans"; consequently, MacArthur received no award at all.[28]

Figure 2: *Brigadier General MacArthur holding a crop at a French chateau, September 1918*

World War I

Rainbow Division

MacArthur returned to the War Department, where he was promoted to major on 11 December 1915. In June 1916, he was assigned as head of the Bureau of Information at the office of the Secretary of War, Newton D. Baker. MacArthur has since been regarded as the Army's first press officer. Following the declaration of war on Germany on 6 April 1917, Baker and MacArthur secured an agreement from President Wilson for the use of the National Guard on the Western Front. MacArthur suggested sending first a division organized from units of different states, so as to avoid the appearance of favoritism toward any particular state. Baker approved the creation of this formation, which became the 42nd ("Rainbow") Division, and appointed Major General William A. Mann, the head of the National Guard Bureau, as its commander; MacArthur was its chief of staff, with the rank of colonel. At MacArthur's request, this commission was in the infantry rather than the engineers.[29]

The 42nd Division was assembled in August and September 1917 at Camp Mills, New York, where its training emphasized open-field combat rather than trench warfare. It sailed in a convoy from Hoboken, New Jersey, for France on 18 October 1917. On 19 December, Mann was replaced as division commander by Major General Charles T. Menoher.[30]

Champagne-Marne Offensive

The 42nd Division entered the line in the quiet Lunéville sector in February 1918. On 26 February, MacArthur and Captain Thomas T. Handy accompanied a French trench raid in which MacArthur assisted in the capture of a number of German prisoners. The commander of the French VII Corps, Major General Georges de Bazelaire, decorated MacArthur with the *Croix de Guerre*. Menoher recommended MacArthur for a Silver Star, which he later received.[31] The Silver Star Medal was not instituted until 8 August 1932, but small Silver Citation Stars were authorized to be worn on the campaign ribbons of those cited in orders for gallantry, similar to the British mention in despatches.[32] When the Silver Star Medal was instituted, it was retroactively awarded to those who had been awarded Silver Citation Stars.[33] On 9 March, the 42nd Division launched three raids of its own on German trenches in the Salient du Feys. MacArthur accompanied a company of the 168th Infantry. This time, his leadership was rewarded with the Distinguished Service Cross. A few days later, MacArthur, who was strict about his men carrying their gas masks but often neglected to bring his own, was gassed. He recovered in time to show Secretary Baker around the area on 19 March.[34]

MacArthur was promoted to brigadier general on 26 June.[35] In late June, the 42nd Division was shifted to Châlons-en-Champagne to oppose the impending German Champagne-Marne Offensive. *Général d'Armée* Henri Gouraud of the French Fourth Army elected to meet the attack with a defense in depth, holding the front line area as thinly as possible and meeting the German attack on his second line of defense. His plan succeeded, and MacArthur was awarded a second Silver Star.[36] The 42nd Division participated in the subsequent Allied counter-offensive, and MacArthur was awarded a third Silver Star on 29 July. Two days later, Menoher relieved Brigadier General Robert A. Brown of the 84th Infantry Brigade of his command, and replaced him with MacArthur. Hearing reports that the enemy had withdrawn, MacArthur went forward on 2 August to see for himself.[37] He later wrote: <templatestyles src="Template:Quote/styles.css"/>

> *It was 3:30 that morning when I started from our right at Sergy. Taking runners from each outpost liaison group to the next, moving by way of what had been No Man's Land, I will never forget that trip. The dead were so thick in spots we tumbled over them. There must have been at least 2,000 of those sprawled bodies. I identified the insignia of six of the best German divisions. The stench was suffocating. Not a tree was standing. The moans and cries of wounded men sounded everywhere. Sniper bullets sung like*

Figure 3: *General Pershing (second from left) decorates Brigadier General MacArthur (third from left) with the Distinguished Service Cross. Major General Charles T. Menoher (left) reads out the citation while Colonel George E. Leach (fourth from left) and Lieutenant Colonel William Joseph Donovan await their decorations.*

> *the buzzing of a hive of angry bees. An occasional shellburst always drew an angry oath from my guide. I counted almost a hundred disabled guns various size and several times that number of abandoned machine guns.*[38]

MacArthur reported back to Menoher and Lieutenant General Hunter Liggett that the Germans had indeed withdrawn, and was awarded a fourth Silver Star.[39] He was also awarded a second *Croix de guerre* and made a *commandeur* of the *Légion d'honneur*.[40]

Battle of Saint-Mihiel and Meuse-Argonne Offensive

The 42nd Division earned a few weeks rest,[41] returning to the line for the Battle of Saint-Mihiel on 12 September 1918. The Allied advance proceeded rapidly and MacArthur was awarded a fifth Silver Star for his leadership of the 84th Infantry Brigade.[42] He received a sixth Silver Star for his participation in a raid on the night of 25–26 September. The 42nd Division was relieved on the night of 30 September and moved to the Argonne sector where it relieved the 1st Division on the night of 11 October. On a reconnaissance the next day, MacArthur was gassed again, earning a second Wound Chevron.[43]

The 42nd Division's participation in the Meuse-Argonne Offensive began on 14 October when it attacked with both brigades. That evening, a conference was called to discuss the attack, during which Charles Pelot Summerall, commander of the First Infantry Division and V Corps, telephoned and demanded that Châtillon be taken by 18:00 the next evening. An aerial photograph had been obtained that showed a gap in the German barbed wire to the northeast of Châtillon. Lieutenant Colonel Walter E. Bare—the commander of the 167th Infantry—proposed an attack from that direction, where the defenses seemed least imposing, covered by a machine-gun barrage. MacArthur adopted this plan.[44] He was wounded, but not severely, while verifying the existence of the gap in the barbed wire.[45]

Summerall nominated MacArthur for the Medal of Honor and promotion to major general, but he received neither.[46] Instead he was awarded a second Distinguished Service Cross.[47] The 42nd Division returned to the line for the last time on the night of 4–5 November 1918.[48] In the final advance on Sedan. MacArthur later wrote that this operation "narrowly missed being one of the great tragedies of American history".[49] An order to disregard unit boundaries led to units crossing into each other's zones. In the resulting chaos, MacArthur was taken prisoner by men of the 1st Division, who mistook him for a German general.[50] His performance in the attack on the Meuse heights led to his being awarded a seventh Silver Star. On 10 November, a day before the armistice that ended the fighting, MacArthur was appointed commander of the 42nd Division. For his service as chief of staff and commander of the 84th Infantry Brigade, he was awarded the Distinguished Service Medal.[51]

His period in command was brief, for on 22 November he, like other brigadier generals, was replaced, and returned to the 84th Infantry Brigade. The 42nd Division was chosen to participate in the occupation of the Rhineland, occupying the Ahrweiler district.[52] In April 1919, they entrained for Brest and Saint-Nazaire, where they boarded ships to return to the United States. MacArthur traveled on the ocean liner SS *Leviathan*, which reached New York on 25 April 1919.[53]

Between the wars

Superintendent of the United States Military Academy

In 1919, MacArthur became Superintendent of the U.S. Military Academy at West Point, which Chief of Staff Peyton March felt had become out of date in many respects and was much in need of reform.[54] Accepting the post allowed MacArthur to retain his rank of brigadier general, instead of being reduced to his substantive rank of major like many of his contemporaries.[55] When MacArthur moved into the superintendent's house with his mother in

Figure 4: *MacArthur as West Point Superintendent*

June 1919,[56] he became the youngest superintendent since Sylvanus Thayer in 1817.[57] However, whereas Thayer had faced opposition from outside the Army, MacArthur had to overcome resistance from graduates and the academic board.[58] MacArthur's vision of what was required of an officer came not just from his recent experience of combat in France but also from that of the occupation of the Rhineland in Germany. The military government of the Rhineland had required the Army to deal with political, economic and social problems but he had found that many West Point graduates had little or no knowledge of fields outside of the military sciences.[56] During the war, West Point had been reduced to an officer candidate school, with five classes graduated in two years. Cadet and staff morale was low and hazing "at an all-time peak of viciousness".[59] MacArthur's first change turned out to be the easiest. Congress had set the length of the course at three years. MacArthur was able to get the four-year course restored.[60]

During the debate over the length of the course, *The New York Times* brought up the issue of the cloistered and undemocratic nature of student life at West Point.[60] Also, starting with Harvard University in 1869, civilian universities had begun grading students on academic performance alone, but West Point had retained the old "whole man" concept of education. MacArthur sought to modernize the system, expanding the concept of military character to include bearing, leadership, efficiency and athletic performance. He formalized the hitherto unwritten Cadet Honor Code in 1922 when he formed the Cadet Honor Committee to review alleged code violations. Elected by the cadets themselves, it had no authority to punish, but acted as a kind of grand jury, reporting offenses to the commandant.[61] MacArthur attempted to end hazing by using officers rather than upperclassmen to train the plebes.[62]

Instead of the traditional summer camp at Fort Clinton, MacArthur had the cadets trained to use modern weapons by regular army sergeants at Fort Dix; they then marched back to West Point with full packs.[62] He attempted to modernize the curriculum by adding liberal arts, government and economics courses, but encountered strong resistance from the Academic Board. In Military Art classes, the study of the campaigns of the American Civil War was replaced with the study of those of World War I. In History class, more emphasis was placed on the Far East. MacArthur expanded the sports program, increasing the number of intramural sports and requiring all cadets to participate.[63] He allowed upper class cadets to leave the reservation, and sanctioned a cadet newspaper, *The Brag*, forerunner of today's *West Pointer*. He also permitted cadets to travel to watch their football team play, and gave them an allowance of $5 ($70 in modern dollars[64]) a month. Professors and alumni alike protested these radical moves.[62] Most of MacArthur's West Point reforms were soon discarded but, in the ensuing years, his ideas became accepted and his innovations were gradually restored.[65]

Army's youngest major general

MacArthur became romantically involved with socialite and multi-millionaire heiress Louise Cromwell Brooks. They were married at her family's villa in Palm Beach, Florida on 14 February 1922. Rumors circulated that General Pershing, who had also courted Louise, had threatened to exile them to the Philippines if they were married. Pershing denied this as "all damn poppycock".[66] In October 1922, MacArthur left West Point and sailed to the Philippines with Louise and her two children, Walter and Louise, to assume command of the Military District of Manila.[67] MacArthur was fond of the children, and spent much of his free time with them.[68]

The revolts in the Philippines had been suppressed, the islands were peaceful now, and in the wake of the Washington Naval Treaty, the garrison was being reduced.[69] MacArthur's friendships with Filipinos like Manuel Quezon offended some people. "The old idea of colonial exploitation", he later conceded, "still had its vigorous supporters."[70] In February and March 1923 MacArthur returned to Washington to see his mother, who was ill from a heart ailment. She recovered, but it was the last time he saw his brother Arthur, who died suddenly from appendicitis in December 1923. In June 1923, MacArthur assumed command of the 23rd Infantry Brigade of the Philippine Division.

On 7 July 1924, he was informed that a mutiny had broken out amongst the Philippine Scouts over grievances concerning pay and allowances. Over 200 were arrested and there were fears of an insurrection. MacArthur was able to calm the situation, but his subsequent efforts to improve the salaries of Filipino troops were frustrated by financial stringency and racial prejudice. On 17 January 1925, at the age of 44, he was promoted, becoming the Army's youngest major general.[71]

Returning to the U.S., MacArthur took command of the IV Corps Area, based at Fort McPherson in Atlanta, Georgia, on 2 May 1925.[72] However, he encountered southern prejudice because he was the son of a Union Army officer, and requested to be relieved.[73] A few months later, he assumed command of the III Corps area, based at Fort McHenry in Baltimore, Maryland, which allowed MacArthur and Louise to move to her Rainbow Hill estate near Garrison, Maryland.[72] However, this relocation also led to what he later described as "one of the most distasteful orders I ever received":[74] a direction to serve on the court martial of Brigadier General Billy Mitchell. MacArthur was the youngest of the thirteen judges, none of whom had aviation experience. Three of them, including Summerall, the president of the court, were removed when defense challenges revealed bias against Mitchell. Despite MacArthur's claim that he had voted to acquit, Mitchell was found guilty as charged and convicted.[72] MacArthur felt "that a senior officer should not be silenced for being at variance with his superiors in rank and with accepted doctrine".[74]

In 1927, MacArthur and Louise separated, and she moved to New York City.[75] In August that year, William C. Prout—the president of the American Olympic Committee—died suddenly and the committee elected MacArthur as their new president. His main task was to prepare the U.S. team for the 1928 Summer Olympics in Amsterdam.[76] MacArthur saw the team as representatives of the United States, and its task was to win medals. "We have not come 3,000 miles", he told them, "just to lose gracefully."[77] The Americans had a successful meet, earning 24 gold medals, and setting 17 Olympic records and seven world records.[78] Upon returning to the U.S., MacArthur received orders to assume command of the Philippine Department.[76] In 1929, while he was in Manila, Louise obtained a divorce, ostensibly on the grounds of "failure to provide". In view of Louise's great wealth, William Manchester described this legal fiction as "preposterous".[79]

Chief of Staff

By 1930, MacArthur was still, at age 50, the youngest of the U.S. Army's major generals, and the best known. He left the Philippines on 19 September 1930 and for a brief time was in command of the IX Corps Area in San Francisco. On 21 November, he was sworn in as Chief of Staff of the United States

Army, with the rank of general.[80] While in Washington, he would ride home each day to have lunch with his mother. At his desk, he would wear a Japanese ceremonial kimono, cool himself with an oriental fan, and smoke cigarettes in a jeweled cigarette holder. In the evenings, he liked to read military history books. About this time, he began referring to himself as "MacArthur".[81] He had already hired a public relations staff to promote his image with the American public, together with a set of ideas he was known to favor, namely: a belief that America needed a strongman leader to deal with the possibility that Communists might lead all of the great masses of unemployed into a revolution; that America's destiny was in the Asia-Pacific region; and a strong hostility to the British Empire.[82] One contemporary described MacArthur as the greatest actor to ever serve as a U.S Army general while another wrote that MacArthur had a court rather than a staff.[83]

The onset of the Great Depression forced Congress to make cuts in the Army's personnel and budget. Some 53 bases were closed, but MacArthur managed to prevent attempts to reduce the number of regular officers from 12,000 to 10,000.[84] MacArthur's main programs included the development of new mobilization plans. He grouped the nine corps areas together under four armies, which were charged with responsibility for training and frontier defense.[85] He also negotiated the MacArthur-Pratt agreement with the Chief of Naval Operations, Admiral William V. Pratt. This was the first of a series of inter-service agreements over the following decades that defined the responsibilities of the different services with respect to aviation. This agreement placed coastal air defense under the Army. In March 1935, MacArthur activated a centralized air command, General Headquarters Air Force, under Major General Frank M. Andrews.[86]

One of MacArthur's most controversial acts came in 1932, when the "Bonus Army" of veterans converged on Washington. He sent tents and camp equipment to the demonstrators, along with mobile kitchens, until an outburst in Congress caused the kitchens to be withdrawn. MacArthur was concerned that the demonstration had been taken over by communists and pacifists but the General Staff's intelligence division reported that only three of the march's 26 key leaders were communists. MacArthur went over contingency plans for civil disorder in the capital. Mechanized equipment was brought to Fort Myer, where anti-riot training was conducted.[87]

On 28 July 1932, a clash between the District police and demonstrators resulted in two men being shot. President Herbert Hoover ordered MacArthur to "surround the affected area and clear it without delay".[88] MacArthur brought up troops and tanks and, against the advice of Major Dwight D. Eisenhower, decided to accompany the troops, although he was not in charge of the operation. The troops advanced with bayonets and sabers drawn under a shower of

Figure 5: *Bonus Army marchers confront the police*

bricks and rocks, but no shots were fired. In less than four hours, they cleared the Bonus Army's campground using tear gas. The gas canisters started a number of fires, causing the only death during the riots. While not as violent as other anti-riot operations, it was nevertheless a public relations disaster.[89] However, the defeat of the "Bonus Army" while unpopular with the American people at large, did make MacArthur into the hero of the more right-wing elements in the Republican Party who believed that the general had saved America from a communist revolution in 1932.[82]

In 1934, MacArthur sued journalists Drew Pearson and Robert S. Allen for defamation after they described his treatment of the Bonus marchers as "unwarranted, unnecessary, insubordinate, harsh and brutal".[90] In turn, they threatened to call Isabel Rosario Cooper as a witness. MacArthur had met Isabel, a Eurasian woman, while in the Philippines, and she had become his mistress. MacArthur was forced to settle out of court, secretly paying Pearson $15,000.[91]

President Hoover was defeated in the 1932 election by Franklin D. Roosevelt. MacArthur and Roosevelt had worked together before World War I and, despite political differences, remained friends. MacArthur supported the New Deal through the Army's operation of the Civilian Conservation Corps. He ensured that detailed plans were drawn up for its employment and decentralized its administration to the corps areas, which became an important factor

Figure 6: *CCC workers construct a road*

in the program's success.[92] MacArthur's support for a strong military, and his public criticism of pacifism and isolationism,[93] made him unpopular with the Roosevelt administration.[94]

Perhaps the most incendiary exchange between Roosevelt and MacArthur occurred over an administration proposal to cut 51% of the Army's budget. In response, MacArthur lectured Roosevelt that "when we lost the next war, and an American boy, lying in the mud with an enemy bayonet through his belly and an enemy foot on his dying throat, spat out his last curse, I wanted the name not to be MacArthur, but Roosevelt". In response, Roosevelt yelled "you must not talk that way to the President!" MacArthur offered to resign, but Roosevelt refused his request, and MacArthur then staggered out of the White House and vomited on the front steps.[95]

In spite of such exchanges, MacArthur was extended an extra year as chief of staff, and ended his tour in October 1935.[94] For his service as chief of staff, he was awarded a second Distinguished Service Medal. He was retroactively awarded two Purple Hearts for his World War I service,[96] a decoration that he authorized in 1932 based loosely on the defunct Military Badge of Merit. MacArthur also insisted on being the first recipient of the Purple Heart, which he had engraved with "#1".[97,98]

Figure 7: *Ceremony at Camp Murphy, 15 August 1941, marking the induction of the Philippine Army Air Corps. Behind MacArthur, from left to right, are Lieutenant Colonel Richard K. Sutherland, Colonel Harold H. George, Lieutenant Colonel William F. Marquat and Major LeGrande A. Diller.*

Field Marshal of the Philippine Army

When the Commonwealth of the Philippines achieved semi-independent status in 1935, President of the Philippines Manuel Quezon asked MacArthur to supervise the creation of a Philippine Army. Quezon and MacArthur had been personal friends since the latter's father had been Governor-General of the Philippines, 35 years earlier. With President Roosevelt's approval, MacArthur accepted the assignment. It was agreed that MacArthur would receive the rank of field marshal, with its salary and allowances, in addition to his major general's salary as Military Advisor to the Commonwealth Government of the Philippines.[99] It would be his fifth tour in the Far East. MacArthur sailed from San Francisco on the SS *President Hoover* in October 1935,[100] accompanied by his mother and sister-in-law. He brought Eisenhower and Major James B. Ord along as his assistants.[101] Another passenger on the *President Hoover* was Jean Marie Faircloth, an unmarried 37-year-old socialite. Over the next two years, MacArthur and Faircloth were frequently seen together.[102] His mother became gravely ill during the voyage and died in Manila on 3 December 1935.[103]

President Quezon officially conferred the title of field marshal on MacArthur in a ceremony at Malacañan Palace on 24 August 1936, and presented him with a gold baton and a unique uniform.[104] The Philippine Army was formed from conscription. Training was conducted by a regular cadre, and the Philippine Military Academy was created along the lines of West Point to train officers.[105] MacArthur and Eisenhower found that few of the training camps had been constructed and the first group of 20,000 trainees did not report until early 1937.[106] Equipment and weapons were "more or less obsolete" American cast offs, and the budget of six million was completely inadequate.[105] MacArthur's requests for equipment fell on deaf ears, although MacArthur and his naval advisor, Lieutenant Colonel Sidney L. Huff, persuaded the Navy to initiate the development of the PT boat.[107] Much hope was placed in the Philippine Army Air Corps, but the first squadron was not organized until 1939.[108]

MacArthur married Jean Faircloth in a civil ceremony on 30 April 1937.[109] Their marriage produced a son, Arthur MacArthur IV, who was born in Manila on 21 February 1938.[110] On 31 December 1937, MacArthur officially retired from the Army. He ceased to represent the U.S. as military adviser to the government, but remained as Quezon's adviser in a civilian capacity.[111] Eisenhower returned to the U.S., and was replaced as MacArthur's chief of staff by Lieutenant Colonel Richard K. Sutherland, while Richard J. Marshall became deputy chief of staff.[112]

World War II

Philippines Campaign (1941–42)

On 26 July 1941, Roosevelt federalized the Philippine Army, recalled MacArthur to active duty in the U.S. Army as a major general, and named him commander of U.S. Army Forces in the Far East (USAFFE). MacArthur was promoted to lieutenant general the following day,[113] and then to general on 20 December.[114] On 31 July 1941, the Philippine Department had 22,000 troops assigned, 12,000 of whom were Philippine Scouts. The main component was the Philippine Division, under the command of Major General Jonathan M. Wainwright.[115] The initial American plan for the defense of the Philippines called for the main body of the troops to retreat to the Bataan peninsula in Manila Bay to hold out against the Japanese until a relief force could arrive.[116] MacArthur changed this plan to one of attempting to hold all of Luzon and using B-17 Flying Fortresses to sink Japanese ships that approached the islands.[117] MacArthur persuaded the decision-makers in Washington that his plans represented the best deterrent to prevent Japan from choosing war and of winning a war if worse did come to worse.[117]

Between July and December 1941, the garrison received 8,500 reinforcements.[118] After years of parsimony, much equipment was shipped. By

Figure 8: *26th Cavalry (Philippine Scouts) move into Pozorrubio past an M3 Stuart tank*

November, a backlog of 1,100,000 shipping tons of equipment intended for the Philippines had accumulated in U.S. ports and depots awaiting vessels.[119] In addition, the Navy intercept station in the islands, known as Station CAST, had an ultra secret Purple cipher machine, which decrypted Japanese diplomatic messages, and partial codebooks for the latest JN-25 naval code. Station CAST sent MacArthur its entire output, via Sutherland, the only officer on his staff authorized to see it.[120]

At 03:30 local time on 8 December 1941 (about 09:00 on 7 December in Hawaii),[121] Sutherland learned of the attack on Pearl Harbor and informed MacArthur. At 05:30, the Chief of Staff of the U.S. Army, General George Marshall, ordered MacArthur to execute the existing war plan, Rainbow Five. MacArthur did nothing. On three occasions, the commander of the Far East Air Force, Major General Lewis H. Brereton, requested permission to attack Japanese bases in Formosa, in accordance with prewar intentions, but was denied by Sutherland. Not until 11:00 did Brereton speak with MacArthur about it, and obtained permission.[122] MacArthur later denied having the conversation.[123] At 12:30, nine hours after the attack on Pearl Harbor, aircraft of Japan's 11th Air Fleet achieved complete tactical surprise when they attacked Clark Field and the nearby fighter base at Iba Field, and destroyed or disabled 18 of Far East Air Force's 35 B-17s, 53 of its 107 P-40s, three P-35s, and more than 25 other aircraft. Most were destroyed on the ground. Substantial damage was done to the bases, and casualties totaled 80 killed and 150

Figure 9: *MacArthur (center) with his Chief of Staff, Major General Richard K. Sutherland, in the Headquarters tunnel on Corregidor, Philippines, on 1 March 1942*

wounded.[124] What was left of the Far East Air Force was all but destroyed over the next few days.[125]

MacArthur attempted to slow the Japanese advance with an initial defense against the Japanese landings. MacArthur's plan for holding all of Luzon against the Japanese collapsed as it spread out the American-Filipino forces too thin.[126] However, he reconsidered his confidence in the ability of his Filipino troops after the Japanese landing force made a rapid advance after landing at Lingayen Gulf on 21 December,[127] and ordered a retreat to Bataan.[128] Within two days of the Japanese landing at Lingayen Gulf, MacArthur had reverted to pre-July 1941 plan of attempting to hold only Bataan while waiting for a relief force to come.[126] Most of the American and some of the Filipino troops were able to retreat back to Baatan, but without most of their supplies, which were abandoned in the confusion.[129] Manila was declared an open city at midnight on 24 December, without any consultation with Admiral Thomas C. Hart, commanding the Asiatic Fleet, forcing the Navy to destroy considerable amounts of valuable material.[130]

On the evening of 24 December, MacArthur moved his headquarters to the island fortress of Corregidor in Manila Bay arriving at 21:30, with his headquarters reporting to Washington as being open on the 25th.[131,132] A series of

Figure 10: *Plaque affixed to MacArthur barracks at the U.S. Military Academy, inscribed with MacArthur's Medal of Honor citation.*

air raids by the Japanese destroyed all the exposed structures on the island and USAFFE headquarters was moved into the Malinta Tunnel. Later, most of the headquarters moved to Bataan, leaving only the nucleus with MacArthur.[133] The troops on Bataan knew that they had been written off but continued to fight. Some blamed Roosevelt and MacArthur for their predicament. A ballad sung to the tune of "The Battle Hymn of the Republic" called him "Dugout Doug".[134] However, most clung to the belief that somehow MacArthur "would reach down and pull something out of his hat".[135]

On 1 January 1942, MacArthur accepted $500,000 from President Quezon of the Philippines as payment for his pre-war service. MacArthur's staff members also received payments: $75,000 for Sutherland, $45,000 for Richard Marshall, and $20,000 for Huff.[136,137] Eisenhower—after being appointed Supreme Commander Allied Expeditionary Force (AEF)—was also offered money by Quezon, but declined.[138] These payments were known only to a few in Manila and Washington, including President Roosevelt and Secretary of War Henry L. Stimson, until they were made public by historian Carol Petillo in 1979. While the payments had been fully legal, the revelation tarnished MacArthur's reputation.

Escape to Australia and Medal of Honor

In February 1942, as Japanese forces tightened their grip on the Philippines, MacArthur was ordered by President Roosevelt to relocate to Australia.[139] On the night of 12 March 1942, MacArthur and a select group that included his wife Jean, son Arthur, and Arthur's Cantonese *amah*, Ah Cheu, fled Corregidor. MacArthur and his party reached Del Monte Airfield on Mindanao, where B-17s picked them up, and flew them to Australia.[140,141] His famous speech, in which he said, "I came through and I shall return", was first made on Terowie railway station in South Australia, on 20 March. Washington asked MacArthur to amend his promise to "We shall return". He ignored the request.

Bataan surrendered on 9 April,[142] and Corregidor on 6 May.[143] George Marshall decided that MacArthur would be awarded the Medal of Honor, a decoration for which he had twice previously been nominated, "to offset any propaganda by the enemy directed at his leaving his command".[144] Eisenhower pointed out that MacArthur had not actually performed any acts of valor as required by law, but Marshall cited the 1927 award of the medal to Charles Lindbergh as a precedent. Special legislation had been passed to authorize Lindbergh's medal, but while similar legislation was introduced authorizing the medal for MacArthur by Congressmen J. Parnell Thomas and James E. Van Zandt, Marshall felt strongly that a serving general should receive the medal from the President and the War Department.[145] MacArthur chose to accept it on the basis that "this award was intended not so much for me personally as it is a recognition of the indomitable courage of the gallant army which it was my honor to command".[146] Arthur and Douglas MacArthur thus became the first father and son to be awarded the Medal of Honor. They remained the only pair until 2001, when Theodore Roosevelt was awarded posthumously for his service during the Spanish–American War, Theodore Roosevelt, Jr. having received one posthumously for his service during World War II. MacArthur's citation, written by George Marshall,[147] read:<templatestyles src="Template:Quote/styles.css"/>

> *For conspicuous leadership in preparing the Philippine Islands to resist conquest, for gallantry and intrepidity above and beyond the call of duty in action against invading Japanese forces, and for the heroic conduct of defensive and offensive operations on the Bataan Peninsula. He mobilized, trained, and led an army which has received world acclaim for its gallant defense against a tremendous superiority of enemy forces in men and arms. His utter disregard of personal danger under heavy fire and aerial bombardment, his calm judgment in each crisis, inspired his troops, galvanized the spirit of resistance of the Filipino people, and confirmed the faith of the American people in their Armed Forces.*

As the symbol of the forces resisting the Japanese, MacArthur received many other accolades. The Native American tribes of the Southwest chose him as a "Chief of Chiefs", which he acknowledged as from "my oldest friends, the companions of my boyhood days on the Western frontier".[148] He was touched when he was named Father of the Year for 1942, and wrote to the National Father's Day Committee that:<templatestyles src="Template:Quote/styles.css"/>

> *By profession I am a soldier and take pride in that fact, but I am prouder, infinitely prouder to be a father. A soldier destroys in order to build; the father only builds, never destroys. The one has the potentialities of death; the other embodies creation and life. And while the hordes of death are mighty, the battalions of life are mightier still. It is my hope that my son when I am gone will remember me, not from battle, but in the home, repeating with him our simple daily prayer, "Our father, Who art in Heaven."*[148]

New Guinea Campaign

General Headquarters

On 18 April 1942, MacArthur was appointed Supreme Commander of Allied Forces in the Southwest Pacific Area (SWPA). Lieutenant General George Brett became Commander, Allied Air Forces, and Vice Admiral Herbert F. Leary became Commander, Allied Naval Forces.[149] Since the bulk of land forces in the theater were Australian, George Marshall insisted an Australian be appointed as Commander, Allied Land Forces, and the job went to General Sir Thomas Blamey. Although predominantly Australian and American, MacArthur's command also included small numbers of personnel from the Netherlands East Indies, the United Kingdom, and other countries.[150]

MacArthur established a close relationship with the Prime Minister of Australia, John Curtin, and was probably the second most-powerful person in the country after the prime minister, although many Australians resented MacArthur as a foreign general who had been imposed upon them.[151] MacArthur had little confidence in Brett's abilities as commander of Allied Air Forces,[149,152,153] and in August 1942 selected Major General George C. Kenney to replace him.[154,155] Kenney's application of air power in support of Blamey's troops would prove crucial.[156]

The staff of MacArthur's General Headquarters (GHQ) was built around the nucleus that had escaped from the Philippines with him, who became known as the "Bataan Gang".[157] Though Roosevelt and George Marshall pressed for Dutch and Australian officers to be assigned to GHQ, the heads of all the staff divisions were American and such officers of other nationalities as were assigned served under them.[150] Initially located in Melbourne,[158] GHQ moved

Figure 11: *Australian Prime Minister John Curtin (right) confers with MacArthur*

to Brisbane—the northernmost city in Australia with the necessary communications facilities—in July 1942,[159] occupying the Australian Mutual Provident Society building (renamed after the war as MacArthur Chambers).[160]

MacArthur formed his own signals intelligence organization, known as the Central Bureau, from Australian intelligence units and American cryptanalysts who had escaped from the Philippines.[161] This unit forwarded Ultra information to Willoughby for analysis.[162] After a press release revealed details of the Japanese naval dispositions during the Battle of the Coral Sea, at which a Japanese attempt to capture Port Moresby was turned back,[163] Roosevelt ordered that censorship be imposed in Australia, and the Advisory War Council granted GHQ censorship authority over the Australian press. Australian newspapers were restricted to what was reported in the daily GHQ communiqué.[163,164] Veteran correspondents considered the communiqués, which MacArthur drafted personally, "a total farce" and "Alice-in-Wonderland information handed out at high level".

Papuan Campaign

Anticipating that the Japanese would strike at Port Moresby again, the garrison was strengthened and MacArthur ordered the establishment of new bases at Merauke and Milne Bay to cover its flanks.[165] The Battle of Midway in June 1942 led to consideration of a limited offensive in the Pacific. MacArthur's

Figure 12: *Senior Allied commanders in New Guinea in October 1942. Left to right: Mr Frank Forde (Australian Minister for the Army); MacArthur; General Sir Thomas Blamey, Allied Land Forces; Lieutenant General George C. Kenney, Allied Air Forces; Lieutenant General Edmund Herring, New Guinea Force; Brigadier General Kenneth Walker, V Bomber Command.*

proposal for an attack on the Japanese base at Rabaul met with objections from the Navy, which favored a less ambitious approach, and objected to an Army general being in command of what would be an amphibious operation. The resulting compromise called for a three-stage advance. The first stage, the seizure of the Tulagi area, would be conducted by the Pacific Ocean Areas, under Admiral Chester W. Nimitz. The later stages would be under MacArthur's command.[166]

The Japanese struck first, landing at Buna in July,[167] and at Milne Bay in August. The Australians repulsed the Japanese at Milne Bay,[168] but a series of defeats in the Kokoda Track campaign had a depressing effect back in Australia. On 30 August, MacArthur radioed Washington that unless action was taken, New Guinea Force would be overwhelmed. He sent Blamey to Port Moresby to take personal command.[169] Having committed all available Australian troops, MacArthur decided to send American forces. The 32nd Infantry Division, a poorly trained National Guard division, was selected.[170] A series of embarrassing reverses in the Battle of Buna–Gona led to outspoken criticism of the

American troops by the Australians. MacArthur then ordered Lieutenant General Robert L. Eichelberger to assume command of the Americans, and "take Buna, or not come back alive".[171,172]

MacArthur moved the advanced echelon of GHQ to Port Moresby on 6 November 1942.[173] After Buna finally fell on 3 January 1943,[174] MacArthur awarded the Distinguished Service Cross to twelve officers for "precise execution of operations". This use of the country's second highest award aroused resentment, because while some, like Eichelberger and George Alan Vasey, had fought in the field, others, like Sutherland and Willoughby, had not.[175] For his part, MacArthur was awarded his third Distinguished Service Medal,[176] and the Australian government had him appointed an honorary Knight Grand Cross of the Order of the Bath.

New Guinea Campaign

At the Pacific Military Conference in March 1943, the Joint Chiefs of Staff approved MacArthur's plan for Operation Cartwheel, the advance on Rabaul.[177] MacArthur explained his strategy: <templatestyles src="Template:Quote/styles.css"/>

> *My strategic conception for the Pacific Theater, which I outlined after the Papuan Campaign and have since consistently advocated, contemplates massive strokes against only main strategic objectives, utilizing surprise and air-ground striking power supported and assisted by the fleet. This is the very opposite of what is termed "island hopping" which is the gradual pushing back of the enemy by direct frontal pressure with the consequent heavy casualties which will certainly be involved. Key points must of course be taken but a wise choice of such will obviate the need for storming the mass of islands now in enemy possession. "Island hopping" with extravagant losses and slow progress ... is not my idea of how to end the war as soon and as cheaply as possible. New conditions require for solution and new weapons require for maximum application new and imaginative methods. Wars are never won in the past.*[178]

In New Guinea, a country without roads, large-scale transportation of men and materiel would have to be accomplished by aircraft or ships. A multi-pronged approach was employed to solve this problem. Disassembled landing craft were shipped to Australia, where they were assembled in Cairns.[179] The range of these small landing craft was to be greatly extended by the landing ships of the VII Amphibious Force, which began arriving in late 1942, and formed part of the newly formed Seventh Fleet.[180] Since the Seventh Fleet had no aircraft carriers, the range of naval operations was limited by that of the fighter aircraft of the Fifth Air Force.[181]

Figure 13: *Conference in Hawaii, July 1944. Left to right: General MacArthur, President Roosevelt, Admiral Leahy, Admiral Nimitz.*

Lieutenant General Walter Krueger's Sixth Army headquarters arrived in SWPA in early 1943 but MacArthur had only three American divisions, and they were tired and depleted from the fighting at Battle of Buna–Gona and Battle of Guadalcanal. As a result, "it became obvious that any military offensive in the South-West Pacific in 1943 would have to be carried out mainly by the Australian Army".[182] The offensive began with the landing at Lae by the Australian 9th Division on 4 September 1943. The next day, MacArthur watched the landing at Nadzab by paratroops of the 503rd Parachute Infantry. His B-17 made the trip on three engines because one failed soon after leaving Port Moresby, but he insisted that it fly on to Nadzab.[183] For this, he was awarded the Air Medal.[184]

The Australian 7th and 9th Divisions converged on Lae, which fell on 16 September. MacArthur advanced his timetable, and ordered the 7th to capture Kaiapit and Dumpu, while the 9th mounted an amphibious assault on Finschhafen. Here, the offensive bogged down, partly because MacArthur had based his decision to assault Finschhafen on Willoughby's assessment that there were only 350 Japanese defenders at Finschhafen, when in fact there were nearly 5,000. A furious battle ensued.[185]

In early November, MacArthur's plan for a westward advance along the coast of New Guinea to the Philippines was incorporated into plans for the war against Japan.[186,187] Three months later, airmen reported no signs of enemy activity in the Admiralty Islands. Although Willoughby did not agree that the islands had been evacuated, MacArthur ordered an amphibious landing there, commencing the Admiralty Islands campaign. He accompanied the assault force aboard the light cruiser *Phoenix*, the flagship of Vice Admiral Thomas C. Kinkaid, the new commander of the Seventh Fleet, and came ashore seven hours after the first wave of landing craft, for which he was awarded the Bronze Star.[188] It took six weeks of fierce fighting before the 1st Cavalry Division captured the islands.[189]

MacArthur had one of the most powerful PR machines of any Allied general during the war, which made him into an extremely popular war hero with the American people.[190] In late 1943–early 1944, there was a serious effort by the conservative faction in the Republican Party centered in the Midwest to have MacArthur seek the Republican nomination to be the candidate for the presidency in the 1944 election, as they regarded the two men most likely to win the Republican nomination, namely Wendell Willkie and Governor Thomas E. Dewey of New York, as too liberal.[190] For a time, MacArthur, who had long seen himself as a potential president, was in the words of the U.S historian Gerhard Weinberg "very interested" in running as the Republican candidate in 1944.[190] However, MacArthur's vow to "return" to the Philippines had not been fulfilled in early 1944 and he decided not to run for president until he had liberated the Philippines.[191]

Furthermore, Weinberg had argued that it is probable that Roosevelt, who knew of the "enormous gratuity" MacArthur had accepted from Quezon in 1942, had used his knowledge of this transaction to blackmail MacArthur into not running for president.[192] Finally, despite the best efforts of the conservative Republicans to put MacArthur's name on the ballot, on April 4, 1944, Governor Dewey won such a convincing victory in the Wisconsin primary (regarded as a significant victory given that the Midwest was a stronghold of the conservative Republicans opposed to Dewey) as to ensure that he would win the Republican nomination to be the GOP's candidate for president in 1944.[191]

MacArthur now bypassed the Japanese forces at Hansa Bay and Wewak, and assaulted Hollandia and Aitape, which Willoughby reported to be lightly defended based on intelligence gathered in the Battle of Sio. MacArthur's bold thrust by going 600 miles up the coast had surprised and confused the Japanese high command, who had not anticipated that MacArthur would take such risks.[193] Although they were out of range of the Fifth Air Force's fighters based in the Ramu Valley, the timing of the operation allowed the aircraft carriers of Nimitz's Pacific Fleet to provide air support.[194] Though risky, the operation turned out to be another success. MacArthur caught the Japanese off balance and cut off Lieutenant General Hatazō Adachi's Japanese XVIII

Army in the Wewak area. Because the Japanese were not expecting an attack, the garrison was weak, and Allied casualties were correspondingly light. However, the terrain turned out to be less suitable for airbase development than first thought, forcing MacArthur to seek better locations further west. While bypassing Japanese forces had great tactical merit, it had the strategic drawback of tying up Allied troops to contain them. Moreover, Adachi was far from beaten, which he demonstrated in the Battle of Driniumor River.[195]

Philippines Campaign (1944–45)

Leyte

In July 1944, President Roosevelt summoned MacArthur to meet with him in Hawaii "to determine the phase of action against Japan". Nimitz made the case for attacking Formosa. MacArthur stressed America's moral obligation to liberate the Philippines. In September, Admiral William Halsey, Jr.'s carriers made a series of air strikes on the Philippines. Opposition was feeble and Halsey concluded, incorrectly, that Leyte was "wide open" and possibly undefended, and recommended that projected operations be skipped in favor of an assault on Leyte.[196]

On 20 October 1944, troops of Krueger's Sixth Army landed on Leyte, while MacArthur watched from the light cruiser USS *Nashville*. That afternoon he arrived off the beach. The advance had not progressed far; snipers were still active and the area was under sporadic mortar fire. When his whaleboat grounded in knee-deep water, MacArthur requested a landing craft, but the beachmaster was too busy to grant his request. MacArthur was compelled to wade ashore.[197] In his prepared speech, he said:<templatestyles src="Template:Quote/styles.css"/>

> *People of the Philippines: I have returned. By the grace of Almighty God our forces stand again on Philippine soil—soil consecrated in the blood of our two peoples. We have come dedicated and committed to the task of destroying every vestige of enemy control over your daily lives, and of restoring upon a foundation of indestructible strength, the liberties of your people.*[198]

Since Leyte was out of range of Kenney's land-based aircraft, MacArthur was dependent on carrier aircraft.[199] Japanese air activity soon increased, with raids on Tacloban, where MacArthur decided to establish his headquarters, and on the fleet offshore. MacArthur enjoyed staying on *Nashville*'s bridge during air raids, although several bombs landed close by, and two nearby cruisers were hit.[200] Over the next few days, the Japanese counterattacked in the Battle of Leyte Gulf, resulting in a near-disaster that MacArthur attributed to the command being divided between himself and Nimitz.[201] Nor did the campaign

Figure 14: *"I have returned" — General MacArthur returns to the Philippines with Philippine President Sergio Osmeña to his right, Philippine Foreign Affairs Secretary Carlos P. Romulo at his rear, and Sutherland on his left. Photo taken by Gaetano Faillace. This iconic image is re-created in larger-than-life statues at MacArthur Landing Memorial National Park*

ashore proceed smoothly. Heavy monsoonal rains disrupted the airbase construction program. Carrier aircraft proved to be no substitute for land-based aircraft, and the lack of air cover permitted the Japanese to pour troops into Leyte. Adverse weather and tough Japanese resistance slowed the American advance, resulting in a protracted campaign.[202,203]

By the end of December, Krueger's headquarters estimated that 5,000 Japanese remained on Leyte, and on 26 December MacArthur issued a communiqué announcing that "the campaign can now be regarded as closed except for minor mopping up". Yet Eichelberger's Eighth Army killed another 27,000 Japanese on Leyte before the campaign ended in May 1945.[204] On 18 December 1944, MacArthur was promoted to the new five-star rank of General of the Army, placing him in the company of Marshall, Eisenhower, Henry "Hap" Arnold, the only four men to achieve the rank in World War II. Including Omar Bradley, MacArthur was one of only five men to achieve the title of General of the Army since the 5 August 1888 death of Philip Sheridan, and he was one of only five American officers to hold the rank as a five-star general. MacArthur was senior to all but Marshall. The rank was created by an Act of Congress when

Figure 15: *General Douglas MacArthur (center), accompanied by Lieutenant Generals George C. Kenney and Richard K. Sutherland and Major General Verne D. Mudge (Commanding General, First Cavalry Division), inspecting the beachhead on Leyte Island, 20 October 1944 with a crowd of onlookers.*

Public Law 78–482 was passed on 14 December 1944,[205] as a temporary rank, subject to reversion to permanent rank six months after the end of the war. The temporary rank was then declared permanent 23 March 1946 by Public Law 333 of the 79th Congress, which also awarded full pay and allowances in the grade to those on the retired list.

Luzon

MacArthur's next move was the invasion of Mindoro, where there were good potential airfield sites. Willoughby estimated, correctly as it turned out, that the island had only about 1,000 Japanese defenders. The problem this time was getting there. Kinkaid balked at sending escort carriers into the restricted waters of the Sulu Sea, and Kenney could not guarantee land based air cover. The operation was clearly hazardous, and MacArthur's staff talked him out of accompanying the invasion on *Nashville*. As the invasion force entered the Sulu Sea, a *kamikaze* struck *Nashville*, killing 133 people and wounding 190 more. Australian and American engineers had three airstrips in operation within two weeks, but the resupply convoys were repeatedly attacked by

Figure 16: *Off Leyte, October 1944 Left to right: Lieutenant General George Kenney, Lieutenant General Richard K. Sutherland, President Sergio Osmeña, General Douglas MacArthur*

kamikazes.[206] During this time, MacArthur quarreled with Sutherland, notorious for his abrasiveness, over the latter's mistress, Captain Elaine Clark. MacArthur had instructed Sutherland not to be bring Clark to Leyte, due to a personal undertaking to Curtin that Australian women on the GHQ staff would not be taken to the Philippines, but Sutherland had brought her along anyway.[207]

The way was now clear for the invasion of Luzon. This time, based on different interpretations of the same intelligence data, Willoughby estimated the strength of General Tomoyuki Yamashita's forces on Luzon at 137,000, while Sixth Army estimated it at 234,000. MacArthur's response was "Bunk!".[208] He felt that even Willoughby's estimate was too high. "Audacity, calculated risk, and a clear strategic aim were MacArthur's attributes",[209] and he disregarded the estimates. In fact, they were too low; Yamashita had more than 287,000 troops on Luzon.[210] This time, MacArthur traveled aboard the light cruiser USS *Boise*, watching as the ship was nearly hit by a bomb and torpedoes fired by midget submarines.[211] His communiqué read: "The decisive battle for the liberation of the Philippines and the control of the Southwest Pacific is at hand. General MacArthur is in personal command at the front and landed with his assault troops."[212]

MacArthur's primary concern was the capture of the port of Manila and the airbase at Clark Field, which were required to support future operations. He urged his commanders on.[213] On 25 January 1945, he moved his advanced headquarters forward to Hacienda Luisita, closer to the front than Krueger's.[214] He ordered the 1st Cavalry Division to conduct a rapid advance on Manila. It reached the northern outskirts of Manila on 3 February,[215] but, unknown to the Americans, Rear Admiral Sanji Iwabuchi had decided to defend Manila to the death. The Battle of Manila raged for the next three weeks.[216] To spare the civilian population, MacArthur prohibited the use of air strikes,[217] but thousands of civilians died in the crossfire or Japanese massacres.[218] He also refused to restrict the traffic of civilians who clogged the roads in and out of Manila, placing humanitarian concerns above military ones except in emergencies.[219] For his part in the capture of Manila, MacArthur was awarded his third Distinguished Service Cross.[220]

After taking Manila, MacArthur installed one of his Filipino friends, Manuel Roxas—who also happened to be one of the few people who knew about the huge sum of money Quezon had given MacArthur in 1942—into a position of power that ensured Roxas was to become the next Filipino president.[221] Roxas had been a leading Japanese collaborator serving in the puppet government of José Laurel, but MacArthur claimed that Roxas had secretly been an American agent all the long.[221] About MacArthur's claim that Roxas was really part of the resistance, the American historian Gerhard Weinberg wrote that "...evidence to this effect has yet to surface", and that by favoring the Japanese collaborator Roxas, MacArthur ensured there was no serious effort to address the issue of Filipino collaboration with the Japanese after the war.[222]

After the Battle of Manila, MacArthur turned his attention to Yamashita, who had retreated into the mountains of central and northern Luzon.[223] Yamashita chose to fight a defensive campaign, being pushed back slowly by Krueger, and was still holding out at the time the war ended, much to MacArthur's intense annoyance as he had wished to liberate the entire Philippines before the war ended.[224] On 2 September 1945, Yamashita (who had a hard time believing that the Emperor had ordered Japan to sign an armistice) came down from the mountains to surrender with some 100,000 of his men.[224]

Southern Philippines

Although MacArthur had no specific directive to do so, and the fighting on Luzon was far from over, he committed his forces to liberate the remainder of the Philippines.[225] In the GHQ communiqué on 5 July, he announced that the Philippines had been liberated and all operations ended, although Yamashita still held out in northern Luzon.[226] Starting in May 1945, MacArthur used his Australian troops in the invasion of Borneo. He accompanied the assault on

Figure 17: *MacArthur signs Japanese surrender instrument aboard USS Missouri. American General Jonathan Wainwright and British General Arthur Percival stand behind him.*

Labuan, and visited the troops ashore. While returning to GHQ in Manila, he visited Davao, where he told Eichelberger that no more than 4,000 Japanese remained alive on Mindanao. A few months later, six times that number surrendered.[227] In July 1945, he was awarded his fourth Distinguished Service Medal.[228]

As part of preparations for Operation Downfall, the invasion of Japan, MacArthur became commander in chief U.S. Army Forces Pacific (AFPAC) in April 1945, assuming command of all Army and Army Air Force units in the Pacific except the Twentieth Air Force. At the same time, Nimitz became commander of all naval forces. Command in the Pacific therefore remained divided.[229] During his planning of the invasion of Japan, MacArthur stressed to the decision-makers in Washington that it was essential to have the Soviet Union enter the war as he argued it was crucial to have the Red Army tie down the Kwantung army in Manchuria.[230] The invasion was pre-empted by the surrender of Japan in August 1945. On 2 September MacArthur accepted the formal Japanese surrender aboard the battleship USS *Missouri*, thus ending hostilities in World War II.[231] In recognition of his role as a maritime strategist, the U.S. Navy awarded him the Navy Distinguished Service Medal.[232]

Figure 18: *MacArthur and the Emperor of Japan, Hirohito, at their first meeting, September 1945*

Occupation of Japan

Protecting the Emperor

On 29 August 1945, MacArthur was ordered to exercise authority through the Japanese government machinery, including the Emperor Hirohito.[233] MacArthur's headquarters was located in the Dai Ichi Life Insurance Building in Tokyo. Unlike in Germany, where the Allies had in May 1945 abolished the German state, the Americans chose to allow the Japanese state to continue to exist, albeit under their ultimate control.[234] Unlike Germany, there was a certain partnership between the occupiers and occupied as MacArthur decided to rule Japan via the Emperor and most of the rest of the Japanese elite.[235] The Emperor was a living god to the Japanese people, and MacArthur found that ruling via the Emperor made his job in running Japan much easier than it otherwise would have been.[236]

MacArthur took the view that a few "militarist" extremists had "hijacked" Japan starting in 1931 with the Mukden Incident, the Emperor was a pro-Western "moderate" who had been powerless to stop the militarists, and thus bore no responsibility for any of the war crimes committed by the Japanese between 1931 and 1945.[236] The American historian Herbert P. Bix described the relationship between the general and the Emperor as: "the Allied commander would use the Emperor, and the Emperor would cooperate in being used. Their relationship became one of expediency and mutual protection, of more political benefit to Hirohito than to MacArthur because Hirohito had more to lose–the entire panoply of symbolic, legitimizing properties of the imperial throne".[237]

At the same time, MacArthur undermined the imperial mystique when his staff released the famous picture of his first meeting with the Emperor, the impact of which on the Japanese public was electric as the Japanese people for the first time saw the Emperor as a mere man overshadowed by the much taller MacArthur instead of the living god he had always been portrayed as. Up to 1945, the Emperor had been a remote, mysterious figure to his people, rarely seen in public and always silent, whose photographs were always taken from a certain angle to make him look taller and more impressive than he really was. No Japanese photographer would have taken such a photo of the Emperor being overshadowed by MacArthur. The Japanese government immediately banned the photo of the Emperor with MacArthur on the grounds that it damaged the imperial mystique, but MacArthur rescinded the ban and ordered all of the Japanese newspapers to print it. The photo was intended as a message to the Emperor about who was going to be the senior partner in their relationship.[238]

As he needed the Emperor, MacArthur protected him from any effort to hold accountable for his actions, and allowed him to issue statements that incorrectly portrayed the emerging democratic post-war era as a continuation of the Meiji era reforms.[239] MacArthur did not allow any investigations of the Emperor, and instead in October 1945 ordered his staff "in the interests of peaceful occupation and rehabilitation of Japan, prevention of revolution and communism, all facts surrounding the execution of the declaration of war and subsequent position of the Emperor which tend to show fraud, menace or duress be marshalled".[240] In January 1946, MacArthur reported to Washington that the Emperor could not be indicted for war crimes on the grounds: <templatestyles src="Template:Quote/styles.css"/>

> *His indictment will unquestionably cause a tremendous convulsion among the Japanese people, the repercussions of which cannot be overestimated. He is a symbol which unites all Japanese. Destroy him and the nation will disintegrate...It is quite possible that a million troops would be required which would have to be maintained for an indefinite number of years.*[241]

To protect the Emperor from being indicted, MacArthur had one of his staff, Brigadier General Bonner Fellers tell the *genrō* Admiral Mitsumasa Yonai on 6 March 1946:<templatestyles src="Template:Quote/styles.css"/>

> *To counter this situation, it would be most convenient if the Japanese side could prove to us that the Emperor is completely blameless. I think the*

forthcoming trials offer the best opportunity to do that. Tojo, in particular should be made to bear all responsibility at his trial. I want you to have Tojo say as follows: "At the imperial conference prior to the start of the war, I already decided to push for war even if his majesty the emperor was against going to war with the United States.'[242]

From the viewpoint of both sides, having one especially evil figure in the form of General Hideki Tojo, on whom everything that went wrong could be blamed, was most politically convenient.[242] At a second meeting on 22 March 1946, Fellers told Admiral Yonai as recorded by his interpreter Mizota Shuichi: <templatestyles src="Template:Quote/styles.css"/>

The most influential advocate of un-American thought in the United States is Cohen (a Jew and a Communist), the top adviser to Secretary of State Byrnes. As I told Yonai... it is extremely disadvantageous to MacArthur's standing in the United States to put on trial the very Emperor who is cooperating with him and facilitating the smooth administration of the occupation. This is the reason for my request... "I wonder whether what I said to Admiral Yonai the other day has already been conveyed to Tojo?".[243]

MacArthur's attempts to shield the Emperor from indictment and to have all the blame taken by General Tojo were successful, which as Herbert P. Bix commented, "...had a lasting and profoundly distorting impact on the Japanese understanding of the lost war".[243]

War crimes trials

MacArthur was responsible for confirming and enforcing the sentences for war crimes handed down by the International Military Tribunal for the Far East.[244] In late 1945, Allied military commissions in various cities of the Orient tried 5,700 Japanese, Taiwanese and Koreans for war crimes. About 4,300 were convicted, almost 1,000 sentenced to death, and hundreds given life imprisonment. The charges arose from incidents that included the Rape of Nanking, the Bataan Death March and Manila massacre.[245] The trial in Manila of Yamashita was criticized because he was hanged for Iwabuchi's Manila massacre, which he had not ordered and of which he was probably unaware.[246] Iwabuchi had killed himself as the battle for Manila was ending.[247]

MacArthur gave immunity to Shiro Ishii and other members of the bacteriological research units in exchange for germ warfare data based on human experimentation.[248] He also exempted the Emperor and all members of the imperial family implicated in war crimes, including Princes such as Chichibu, Asaka, Takeda, Higashikuni and Fushimi, from criminal prosecutions. MacArthur confirmed that the emperor's abdication would not be necessary.[249] In doing so, he ignored the advice of many members of the imperial family and

Figure 19: *The defendants at the Tokyo War Crimes Trials*

Japanese intellectuals who publicly called for the abdication of the Emperor and the implementation of a regency.[250]

Supreme Commander for the Allied Powers

As Supreme Commander for the Allied Powers (SCAP) in Japan, MacArthur and his staff helped Japan rebuild itself, eradicate militarism and ultra-nationalism, promote political civil liberties, institute democratic government, and chart a new course that ultimately made Japan one of the world's leading industrial powers. The U.S. was firmly in control of Japan to oversee its reconstruction, and MacArthur was effectively the interim leader of Japan from 1945 until 1948.[251] In 1946, MacArthur's staff drafted a new constitution that renounced war and stripped the Emperor of his military authority. The constitution—which became effective on 3 May 1947—instituted a parliamentary system of government, under which the Emperor acted only on the advice of his ministers. It included the famous Article 9, which outlawed belligerency as an instrument of state policy and the maintenance of a standing army. The constitution also enfranchised women, guaranteed fundamental human rights, outlawed racial discrimination, strengthened the powers of Parliament and the Cabinet, and decentralized the police and local government.[252]

A major land reform was also conducted, led by Wolf Ladejinsky of MacArthur's SCAP staff. Between 1947 and 1949, approximately 4,700,000 acres (1,900,000 ha), or 38% of Japan's cultivated land, was purchased from the landlords under the government's reform program, and 4,600,000 acres (1,860,000 ha) was resold to the farmers who worked them. By 1950, 89% of all agricultural land was owner-operated and only 11% was tenant-operated.[253] MacArthur's efforts to encourage trade union membership met with phenomenal success, and by 1947, 48% of the non-agricultural workforce was unionized. Some of MacArthur's reforms were rescinded in 1948 when his unilateral control of Japan was ended by the increased involvement of the State Department.[254] During the Occupation, SCAP successfully, if not entirely, abolished many of the financial coalitions known as the Zaibatsu, which had previously monopolized industry.[255] Eventually, looser industrial groupings known as *Keiretsu* evolved. The reforms alarmed many in the U.S. Departments of Defense and State, who believed they conflicted with the prospect of Japan and its industrial capacity as a bulwark against the spread of communism in Asia.[256]

In 1948, MacArthur made a bid to win the Republican nomination to be the GOP candidate for president, which was the most serious of several efforts he made over the years.[257] MacArthur's status as one of America's most popular war heroes together with his reputation as the statesman who had "transformed" Japan gave him a strong basis for running for president, but MacArthur's lack of connections within the GOP were a major handicap.[258] MacArthur's strongest supporters came from the quasi-isolationist, Midwestern wing of the Republicans and embraced men such as Brigadier General Hanford MacNider, Philip La Follette, and Brigadier General Robert E. Wood, a diverse collection of "Old Right" and Progressive Republicans only united by a belief that the U.S. was too much involved in Europe for its own good.[259] MacArthur declined to campaign for the presidency himself, but he privately encouraged his supporters to put his name on the ballot.[260] MacArthur had always stated he would retire when a peace treaty was signed with Japan, and his push in the fall of 1947 to have the U.S sign a peace treaty with Japan was intended to allow him to retire on a high note, and thus campaign for the presidency. For the same reasons, Truman subverted MacArthur's efforts to have peace treaty signed in 1947, saying that more time was needed before the U.S could formally make peace with Japan.[261]

Without a peace treaty, MacArthur decided not to resign while at the same time writing letters to Wood saying he would be more than happy to accept the Republican nomination if it were offered to him.[262] In late 1947 and early 1948, MacArthur received several Republican grandees in Tokyo.[263] On 9 March 1948 MacArthur issued a press statement declaring his interest in being the Republican candidate for president, saying he would be honored if the Republican Party were to nominate him, but would not resign from the Army to campaign for the presidency.[264] The press statement had been forced by Wood, who told MacArthur that it was impossible to campaign for a man who was not officially running for president, and that MacArthur could either declare his candidacy or see Wood cease campaigning for him.[264] MacArthur's supporters made a major effort to win the Wisconsin Republican primary held on 6 April 1948.[265] MacArthur's refusal to campaign badly hurt his chances and it was won to everybody's surprise by Harold Stassen.[266] The defeat in Wisconsin followed by defeat in Nebraska effectively ended MacArthur's chances of winning the Republican nomination, but MacArthur refused to withdraw his name until the 1948 Republican National Convention which was won by Governor Thomas Dewey of New York.[267]

In an address to Congress on 19 April 1951, MacArthur declared: <templatestyles src="Template:Quote/styles.css"/>

> *The Japanese people since the war have undergone the greatest reformation recorded in modern history. With a commendable will, eagerness to learn, and marked capacity to understand, they have from the ashes left in war's wake erected in Japan an edifice dedicated to the supremacy of individual liberty and personal dignity, and in the ensuing process there has been created a truly representative government committed to the advance of political morality, freedom of economic enterprise, and social justice.*[268]

MacArthur handed over power to the Japanese government in 1949, but remained in Japan until relieved by President Harry S. Truman on 11 April 1951. The San Francisco Peace Treaty, signed on 8 September 1951, marked the end of the Allied occupation, and when it went into effect on 28 April 1952, Japan was once again an independent state.[269] The Japanese subsequently gave him the nickname *Gaijin Shogun* ("foreign military ruler") but not until around the time of his death in 1964.[270]

Korean War

South to the Naktong, North to the Yalu

On 25 June 1950, North Korea invaded South Korea, starting the Korean War.[271] The United Nations Security Council passed Resolution 82, which authorized a United Nations (UN) force to assist South Korea.[272] The UN empowered the American government to select a commander, and the Joint Chiefs of Staff unanimously recommended MacArthur.[273] He therefore became Commander-in-Chief of the United Nations Command (UNCOM), while remaining SCAP in Japan and Commander of the USAFFE.[274] All South Korean forces were also placed under his command. As they retreated before the North Korean onslaught, MacArthur received permission to commit U.S.

Figure 20: *MacArthur observes the naval shelling of Inchon from USS Mount McKinley, 15 September 1950 with Brigadier General Courtney Whitney (left) and Major General Edward M. Almond (right).*

ground forces. All the first units to arrive could do was trade men and ground for time, falling back to the Pusan Perimeter.[275] By the end of August, the crisis subsided. North Korean attacks on the perimeter had tapered off. While the North Korean force numbered 88,000 troops, Lieutenant General Walton Walker's Eighth Army now numbered 180,000, and he had more tanks and artillery pieces.[276]

In 1949, the Chairman of the Joint Chiefs of Staff, General of the Army Omar Bradley, had predicted that "large scale combined amphibious operations ... will never occur again", but by July 1950, MacArthur was planning just such an operation.[277] MacArthur compared his plan with that of General James Wolfe at the Battle of the Plains of Abraham, and brushed aside the problems of tides, hydrography and terrain.[278] In September, despite lingering concerns from superiors, MacArthur's soldiers and marines made a successful landing at Inchon, deep behind North Korean lines. Launched with naval and close air support, the landing outflanked the North Koreans, recaptured Seoul and forced them to retreat northward in disarray.[279] Visiting the battlefield on 17 September, MacArthur surveyed six T-34 tanks that had been knocked out by Marines, ignoring sniper fire around him, except to note that the North Korean marksmen were poorly trained.[280]

On 11 September, Truman issued orders for an advance beyond the 38th parallel into North Korea. MacArthur now planned another amphibious assault, on Wonsan on the east coast, but it fell to South Korean troops before the 1st Marine Division could reach it by sea.[281] In October, MacArthur met with Truman at the Wake Island Conference, with Truman emulating Roosevelt's wartime meeting with MacArthur in Hawaii.[282] The president awarded MacArthur his fifth Distinguished Service Medal.[283] Briefly questioned about the Chinese threat, MacArthur dismissed it, saying that he hoped to be able to withdraw the Eighth Army to Japan by Christmas, and to release a division for service in Europe in January. He regarded the possibility of Soviet intervention as a more serious threat.[284]

A month later, things had changed. The enemy were engaged by the UN forces at the Battle of Unsan in late October, which demonstrated the presence of Chinese soldiers in Korea and rendered significant losses to the American and other UN troops. Nevertheless, Willoughby downplayed the evidence about Chinese intervention in the war. He estimated that up to 71,000 Chinese soldiers were in the country, while the true number was closer to 300,000. He was not alone in this miscalculation. On 24 November, the Central Intelligence Agency reported to Truman that while there could be as many as 200,000 Chinese troops in Korea, "there is no evidence that the Chinese Communists plan major offensive operations."[285]

That day, MacArthur flew to Walker's headquarters and he later wrote:<templatestyles src="Template:Quote/styles.css"/>

> *For five hours I toured the front lines. In talking to a group of officers I told them of General Bradley's desire and hope to have two divisions home by Christmas ... What I had seen at the front line worried me greatly. The R.O.K. troops were not yet in good shape, and the entire line was deplorably weak in numbers. If the Chinese were actually in heavy force, I decided I would withdraw our troops and abandon any attempt to move north. I decided to reconnoiter and try to see with my own eyes, and interpret with my own long experience what was going on ...*[286]

MacArthur flew over the front line himself in his Douglas C-54 Skymaster but saw no signs of a Chinese build up and therefore decided to wait before ordering an advance or withdrawal. Evidence of the Chinese activity was hidden to MacArthur: the Chinese Army traveled at night and dug in during the day. For his reconnaissance efforts, MacArthur was nonetheless awarded the Distinguished Flying Cross and honorary combat pilot's wings.[286]

The next day, 25 November 1950, Walker's Eighth Army was attacked by the Chinese Army and soon the UN forces were in retreat. MacArthur provided the Chief of Staff, General J. Lawton Collins with a series of nine successive withdrawal lines.[287] On 23 December, Walker was killed when his jeep collided with a truck, and was replaced by Lieutenant General Matthew B. Ridgway, whom MacArthur had selected in case of such an eventuality.[288] Ridgway noted that MacArthur's "prestige, which had gained an extraordinary luster after Inch'on, was badly tarnished. His credibility suffered in the unforeseen outcome of the November offensive ..."[289]

Collins discussed the possible use of nuclear weapons in Korea with MacArthur in December, and later asked him for a list of targets in the Soviet Union in case it entered the war. MacArthur testified before the Congress in 1951 that he had never recommended the use of nuclear weapons. He did at one point consider a plan to cut off North Korea with radioactive poisons; he did not recommend it at the time, although he later broached the matter with Eisenhower, then president-elect, in 1952. In 1954, in an interview published after his death, he stated he had wanted to drop atomic bombs on enemy bases, but in 1960, he challenged a statement by Truman that he had advocated using atomic bombs. Truman issued a retraction, stating that he had no evidence of the claim; it was merely his personal opinion.[290,291]

In April 1951, the Joint Chiefs of Staff drafted orders for MacArthur authorizing nuclear attacks on Manchuria and the Shantung Peninsula if the Chinese launched airstrikes originating from there against his forces.[292] The next day Truman met with the chairman of the United States Atomic Energy Commission, Gordon Dean,[293] and arranged for the transfer of nine Mark 4 nuclear bombs to military control. Dean was apprehensive about delegating the decision on how they should be used to MacArthur, who lacked expert technical knowledge of the weapons and their effects.[294] The Joint Chiefs were not entirely comfortable about giving them to MacArthur either, for fear that he might prematurely carry out his orders.[292] Instead, they decided that the nuclear strike force would report to the Strategic Air Command.[295]

Removal from command

Within weeks of the Chinese attack, MacArthur was forced to retreat from North Korea.[296] Seoul fell in January 1951, and both Truman and MacArthur were forced to contemplate the prospect of abandoning Korea entirely.[297] European countries did not share MacArthur's world view, distrusted his judgment, and were afraid that he might use his stature and influence with the American public to re-focus American policy away from Europe and towards Asia. They were concerned that this might lead to a major war with China, possibly involving nuclear weapons.[298] Since in February 1950 the Soviet Union and China had signed a defensive alliance committing each to go to war if the other party was attacked, the possibility that an American attack on China

Figure 21: *Douglas MacArthur (rear), Jean MacArthur, and son Arthur MacArthur IV returning to the Philippines for a visit in 1950.*

would cause World War III was considered to be very real at the time. In a visit to the United States in December 1950, the British prime minister, Clement Attlee, had raised the fears of the British and other European governments that "General MacArthur was running the show".[299]

Under Ridgway's command, the Eighth Army pressed north again in January. He inflicted heavy casualties on the Chinese,[300] recaptured Seoul in March 1951, and pushed on to the 38th Parallel.[301] With the improved military situation, Truman now saw the opportunity to offer a negotiated peace but, on 24 March, MacArthur called upon China to admit that it had been defeated, simultaneously challenging both the Chinese and his own superiors. Truman's proposed announcement was shelved.[302]

On 5 April, Representative Joseph William Martin, Jr., the Republican leader in the House of Representatives, read aloud on the floor of the House a letter from MacArthur critical of Truman's Europe-first policy and limited-war strategy.[303] The letter concluded with: <templatestyles src="Template:Quote/styles.css"/>

> *It seems strangely difficult for some to realize that here in Asia is where the communist conspirators have elected to make their play for global conquest, and that we have joined the issue thus raised on the battlefield; that*

> *here we fight Europe's war with arms while the diplomats there still fight it with words; that if we lose the war to communism in Asia the fall of Europe is inevitable, win it and Europe most probably would avoid war and yet preserve freedom. As you pointed out, we must win. There is no substitute for victory.*[304]

In March 1951 secret United States intercepts of diplomatic dispatches disclosed clandestine conversations in which General MacArthur expressed confidence to the Tokyo embassies of Spain and Portugal that he would succeed in expanding the Korean War into a full-scale conflict with the Chinese Communists. When the intercepts came to the attention of President Truman, he was enraged to learn that MacArthur was not only trying to increase public support for his position on conducting the war, but had secretly informed foreign governments that he planned to initiate actions that were counter to United States policy. The President was unable to act immediately since he could not afford to reveal the existence of the intercepts and because of MacArthur's popularity with the public and political support in Congress. However, following the release on April 5 by Representative Martin of MacArthur's letter, Truman concluded he could relieve MacArthur of his commands without incurring unacceptable political damage.[305,306,307]

Truman summoned Secretary of Defense George Marshall, Chairman of the Joint Chiefs Omar Bradley, Secretary of State Dean Acheson and Averell Harriman to discuss what to do about MacArthur.[308] They concurred MacArthur should be relieved of his command, but made no recommendation to do so. Although they felt that it was correct "from a purely military point of view",[309] they were aware that there were important political considerations as well.[309] Truman and Acheson agreed that MacArthur was insubordinate, but the Joint Chiefs avoided any suggestion of this.[310] Insubordination was a military offense, and MacArthur could have requested a public court martial similar to that of Billy Mitchell. The outcome of such a trial was uncertain, and it might well have found him not guilty and ordered his reinstatement.[311] The Joint Chiefs agreed that there was "little evidence that General MacArthur had ever failed to carry out a direct order of the Joint Chiefs, or acted in opposition to an order". "In point of fact", Bradley insisted, "MacArthur had stretched but not legally violated any JCS directives. He had violated the President's 6 December directive [not to make public statements on policy matters], relayed to him by the JCS, but this did not constitute violation of a JCS order."[310] Truman ordered MacArthur's relief by Ridgway, and the order went out on 10 April with Bradley's signature.[312]

In a 3 December 1973 article in *Time* magazine, Truman was quoted as saying in the early 1960s: <templatestyles src="Template:Quote/styles.css"/>

Figure 22: *A euphoric ticker-tape parade for MacArthur took place in Chicago on 26 April 1951. MacArthur is in the second car.*

> *I fired him because he wouldn't respect the authority of the President. I didn't fire him because he was a dumb son of a bitch, although he was, but that's not against the law for generals. If it was, half to three-quarters of them would be in jail.*

The relief of the famous general by the unpopular politician for communicating with Congress led to a constitutional crisis,[313] and a storm of public controversy. Polls showed that the majority of the public disapproved of the decision to relieve MacArthur.[314] By February 1952, almost nine months later, Truman's approval rating had fallen to 22 percent. As of 2014[315], that remains the lowest Gallup Poll approval rating recorded by any serving president.[316] As the increasingly unpopular war in Korea dragged on, Truman's administration was beset with a series of corruption scandals, and he eventually decided not to run for re-election.[317] Beginning on 3 May 1951, a Joint Senate Committee—chaired by Democrat Richard Russell, Jr.—investigated MacArthur's removal. It concluded that "the removal of General MacArthur was within the constitutional powers of the President but the circumstances were a shock to national pride".[318]

Figure 23: *MacArthur speaking at Soldier Field in Chicago in 1951*

Later life

A day after his arrival in San Francisco from Korea on 18 April 1951, MacArthur had flown with his family to Washington, D.C. where he was scheduled to address a joint session of Congress. It was his and Jean's first visit to the continental United States since 1937, when they had been married; Arthur IV, now aged 13, had never been to the U.S.[319] And, on April 19, 1951, MacArthur made his last official appearance in a farewell address to the U.S. Congress presenting and defending his side of his disagreement with Truman over the conduct of the Korean War. During his speech, he was interrupted by fifty ovations.[320] MacArthur ended the address saying: <templatestyles src=”Template:Quote/styles.css”/>

> *I am closing my 52 years of military service. When I joined the Army, even before the turn of the century, it was the fulfillment of all of my boyish hopes and dreams. The world has turned over many times since I took the oath on the plain at West Point, and the hopes and dreams have long since vanished, but I still remember the refrain of one of the most popular barrack ballads of that day which proclaimed most proudly that "old soldiers never die; they just fade away".*
>
> *And like the old soldier of that ballad, I now close my military career and just fade away, an old soldier who tried to do his duty as God gave him the light to see that duty.*

Figure 24: *Douglas MacArthur Memorial in Norfolk, Virginia. The statue is a duplicate of the one at West Point. The base houses a time capsule which contains various MacArthur, Norfolk and MacArthur Foundation memorabilia.*

Good Bye.[321]

MacArthur received public adulation, which aroused expectations that he would run for president, but he was not a candidate. MacArthur carried out a speaking tour in 1951–52 attacking the Truman administration for "appeasement in Asia" and for mismanaging the economy.[322] Initially attracting large crowds, by early 1952 MacArthur's speeches were attracting smaller and smaller numbers of people as many complained that MacArthur seemed more interested in settling scores with Truman and praising himself than in offering up a constructive vision for the nation.[323] MacArthur felt uncomfortable campaigning for the Republican nomination, and hoped that at the Republican convention, a deadlock would ensue between Senator Robert Taft and General Eisenhower, which would end with the GOP nominating him as the best compromise.[324] MacArthur's unwillingness to campaign for the presidency seriously hurt his ability to win the nomination. In the end, MacArthur endorsed Senator Robert A. Taft, and was keynote speaker at the 1952 Republican National Convention. Taft lost the nomination to Eisenhower, who went on to win the 1952 election by a landslide.[325] Once elected, Eisenhower consulted with MacArthur about ending the war in Korea.[326]

Douglas and Jean MacArthur spent their last years together in the penthouse of the Waldorf Towers, a part of the Waldorf-Astoria Hotel.[327] He was elected chairman of the board of Remington Rand. In that year, he earned a salary of $68,000 (equivalent to $612,000 in 2016), in addition to $20,000 pay and allowances as a General of the Army.[328] The Waldorf became the setting for an annual birthday party on 26 January thrown by the general's former deputy chief engineer, Major General Leif J. Sverdrup. At the 1960 celebration for MacArthur's 80th birthday, many of his friends were startled by the general's obviously deteriorating health. The next day, he collapsed and was rushed into surgery at St. Luke's Hospital to control a severely swollen prostate.[329]

After his recovery, MacArthur methodically began to carry out the closing acts of his life. He visited the White House for a final reunion with Eisenhower. In 1961, he made a "sentimental journey" to the Philippines, where he was decorated by President Carlos P. Garcia with the Philippine Legion of Honor. MacArthur also accepted a $900,000 (equivalent to $7.25 million in 2016) advance from Henry Luce for the rights to his memoirs, and wrote the volume that would eventually be published as *Reminiscences*.[329] Sections began to appear in serialized form in *Life magazine* in the months before his death.[330]

President John F. Kennedy solicited MacArthur's counsel in 1961. The first of two meetings was held shortly after the Bay of Pigs Invasion. MacArthur was extremely critical of the military advice given to Kennedy, and cautioned the young President to avoid a U.S. military build-up in Vietnam, pointing out that domestic problems should be given a much greater priority. Shortly before his death, MacArthur gave similar advice to President Lyndon B. Johnson.[331]

In 1962, West Point honored the increasingly frail MacArthur with the Sylvanus Thayer Award for outstanding service to the nation, which had gone to Eisenhower the year before. MacArthur's speech to the cadets in accepting the award had as its theme "Duty, Honor, Country": <templatestyles src="Template:Quote/styles.css"/>

> *The shadows are lengthening for me. The twilight is here. My days of old have vanished, tone and tint. They have gone glimmering through the dreams of things that were. Their memory is one of wondrous beauty, watered by tears, and coaxed and caressed by the smiles of yesterday. I listen vainly, but with thirsty ears, for the witching melody of faint bugles blowing reveille, of far drums beating the long roll. In my dreams I hear again the crash of guns, the rattle of musketry, the strange, mournful mutter of the battlefield. But in the evening of my memory, always I come back to West Point. Always there echoes and re-echoes: Duty, Honor, Country. Today marks my final roll call with you, but I want you to know that when I cross the river my last conscious thoughts will be of The Corps, and The Corps, and The Corps. I bid you farewell.*

Figure 25: *MacArthur's sarcophagus at the MacArthur Memorial in Norfolk*

In 1963, President Kennedy asked MacArthur to help mediate a dispute between the National Collegiate Athletic Association and the Amateur Athletic Union over control of amateur sports in the country. The dispute threatened to derail the participation of the United States in the 1964 Summer Olympics. His presence helped to broker a deal, and participation in the games went on as planned.

Death and legacy

Douglas MacArthur died at Walter Reed Army Medical Center on 5 April 1964, of biliary cirrhosis.[332] Kennedy had authorized a state funeral before his own death in 1963, and Johnson confirmed the directive, ordering that MacArthur be buried "with all the honor a grateful nation can bestow on a departed hero".[333] On 7 April his body was taken to New York City, where it lay in an open casket at the Seventh Regiment Armory for about 12 hours. That night it was taken on a funeral train to Union Station and transported by a funeral procession to the Capitol, where it lay in state. An estimated 150,000 people filed by the bier.[334]

MacArthur had requested to be buried in Norfolk, Virginia, where his mother had been born and where his parents had married. Accordingly, on 11 April, his funeral service was held in St Paul's Episcopal Church in Norfolk and his

Figure 26: *MacArthur commemorative postage stamp*

body was finally laid to rest in the rotunda of the Douglas MacArthur Memorial (the former Norfolk City Hall and later courthouse).[335]

In 1960, the mayor of Norfolk had proposed using funds raised by public contribution to remodel the old Norfolk City Hall as a memorial to General MacArthur and as a repository for his papers, decorations, and mementos he had accepted. Restored and remodeled, the MacArthur Memorial contains nine museum galleries whose contents reflect the general's 50 years of military service. At the heart of the memorial is a rotunda. In its center lies a sunken circular crypt with two marble sarcophagi, one for MacArthur,[336] the other for Jean, who continued to live in the Waldorf Towers until her own death in 2000.

The MacArthur Chambers in Brisbane, Australia, hosts the MacArthur Museum on the 8th floor where MacArthur had his office.

MacArthur has a contested legacy. In the Philippines in 1942, he suffered a defeat that Gavin Long described as "the greatest in the history of American foreign wars".[337] Despite this, "in a fragile period of the American psyche when the general American public, still stunned by the shock of Pearl Harbor and uncertain what lay ahead in Europe, desperately needed a hero, they wholeheartedly embraced Douglas MacArthur—good press copy that he was. There simply were no other choices that came close to matching his mystique, not to mention his evocative lone-wolf stand—something that has always resonated with Americans."

MacArthur's concept of the role of the soldier as encompassing a broad spectrum of roles that included civil affairs, quelling riots and low-level conflict, was dismissed by the majority of officers who had fought in Europe during World War II, and afterwards saw the Army's role as fighting the Soviet Union.[338] Unlike them, in his victories in New Guinea in 1944, the Philippines in 1945 and Korea in 1950, he fought outnumbered, and relied on maneuver and surprise for success.[339] The American Sinologist John Fairbank called MacArthur "our greatest soldier".

On the other hand, Truman once remarked that he did not understand how the US Army could "produce men such as Robert E. Lee, John J. Pershing, Eisenhower and Bradley and at the same time produce Custers, Pattons and MacArthur".[340] His relief of MacArthur cast a long shadow over American civil-military relations for decades. When Lyndon Johnson met with William Westmoreland in Honolulu in 1966, he told him: "General, I have a lot riding on you. I hope you don't pull a MacArthur on me."[341] MacArthur's relief "left a lasting current of popular sentiment that in matters of war and peace, the military really knows best", a philosophy which became known as "MacArthurism".

MacArthur remains a controversial and enigmatic figure. He has been portrayed as a reactionary, although he was in many respects ahead of his time. He championed a progressive approach to the reconstruction of Japanese society, arguing that all occupations ultimately ended badly for the occupier and the occupied. He was often out of step with his contemporaries, such as in 1941 when he contended that Nazi Germany could not defeat the Soviet Union, when he argued that North Korea and China were no mere Soviet puppets, and throughout his career in his insistence that the future lay in the Far East. As such, MacArthur implicitly rejected White American contemporary notions of their own racial superiority. He always treated Filipino and Japanese leaders with respect as equals. At the same time, his Victorian sensibilities recoiled at leveling Manila with aerial bombing, an attitude the hardened World War II generation regarded as old fashioned.[342] When asked about MacArthur, Field Marshal Sir Thomas Blamey once said, "The best and the worst things you hear about him are both true."[343]

Honors and awards

During his lifetime, MacArthur earned over 100 military decorations from the U.S. and other countries including the Medal of Honor, the French *Légion d'honneur* and *Croix de guerre*, the Order of the Crown of Italy, the Order

Figure 27: *West entrance of the MacArthur Tunnel in San Francisco, California*

of Orange-Nassau from the Netherlands, the Honorary Knight Grand Cross of the Order of the Bath from Australia, and the Order of the Rising Sun with Paulownia Flowers, Grand Cordon from Japan.

MacArthur was enormously popular with the American public. Streets, public works, and children were named after him. Even a dance step was named after him.[344] In 1955, his promotion to General of the Armies was proposed in Congress, but the proposal was shelved.[345,346]

Since 1987 the General Douglas MacArthur Leadership Awards are presented annually by the United States Army on behalf of the General Douglas MacArthur Foundation to recognize company grade officers (lieutenants and captains) and junior warrant officers (warrant officer one and chief warrant officer two) who have demonstrated the attributes of "duty, honor, country" in their professional lives and in service to their communities.

The General Douglas MacArthur Foundation presents the MacArthur Cadet Awards in recognition of outstanding cadets within the Association of Military Colleges and Schools of the United States. The MacArthur Award is presented annually to seniors at these military schools. The award is designed to encourage cadets to emulate the leadership qualities shown by General Douglas MacArthur, as a student at West Texas Military Institute and the U.S. Military Academy. Approximately 40 schools are authorized to provide the award to its top cadet each year.

The MacArthur Leadership Award at the Royal Military College of Canada in Kingston, Ontario is awarded to the graduating officer cadet who demonstrates outstanding leadership performance based on the credo of Duty-Honor-Country and potential for future military service.

In popular culture

Several actors have portrayed MacArthur on-screen.

- Dayton Lummis in *The Court-Martial of Billy Mitchell* (1955)
- Henry Fonda in the television movie *Collision Course: Truman vs. MacArthur* (1976)
- Gregory Peck in *MacArthur* (1977)
- Laurence Olivier in *Inchon* (1981)
- John Bennett Perry in *Farewell to the King* (1989)
- James B. Sikking in *In Pursuit of Honor* (1995)
- Daniel von Bargen in *Truman* (1995)
- Robert Dawson in *The Sun* (2005)
- Tommy Lee Jones in *Emperor* (2012)
- Liam Neeson in *Operation Chromite* (2016)
- Michael Ironside in *Tokyo Trial* (2016)

Bibliography

<templatestyles src="Template:Refbegin/styles.css" />

- MacArthur, Douglas (1942). Waldrop, Frank C, ed. *MacArthur on War*. New York: Duell, Sloan and Pearce. OCLC 1163286[347].
- —— (1952). *Revitalizing a Nation; a Statement of Beliefs, Opinions, and Policies Embodied in the Public Pronouncements of Douglas MacArthur*. Chicago: Heritage Foundation. OCLC 456989[348].
- —— (1964). *Reminiscences*. New York: McGraw-Hill. OCLC 562005[349].
- —— (1965). Whan Jr, Vorin E, ed. *A Soldier Speaks; Public Papers and Speeches of General of the Army, Douglas MacArthur*. New York: Praeger. OCLC 456849[350].
- —— (1965). *Courage was the Rule: General Douglas MacArthur's Own Story* (Juvenile audience) (Abridged ed.). New York: McGraw-Hill. OCLC 1307481[351].
- —— (1965). *Duty, Honor, Country; a Pictorial Autobiography* (1st ed.). New York: McGraw-Hill. OCLC 1342695[352].
- —— (1966). Willoughby, Charles A, ed. *Reports of General MacArthur* (4 Volumes). Washington, D.C.: U.S. Government Printing Office. OCLC 407539[353].

References

<templatestyles src="Template:Refbegin/styles.css" />

- Anders, Roger M. (January 1988). "The Atomic Bomb and the Korean War: Gordon Dean and the Issue of Civilian Control". *Military Affairs*. Lexington, Virginia: Society for Military History. **52** (1): 1–6. doi: 10.2307/1988372[354]. JSTOR 1988372[355].
- Bix, Herbert (2000). *Hirohito and the Making of Modern Japan*. New York: HarperCollins. ISBN 0-06-093130-2.
- Casey, Hugh J., ed. (1959). *Volume IV: Amphibian Engineer Operations*. Engineers of the Southwest Pacific 1941–1945. Washington, D.C.: Government Printing Office. OCLC 220327009[356].
- Casey, Steven (2008). *Selling the Korean War: Propaganda, Politics and Public Opinion*. Oxford: Oxford University Press. ISBN 978-0-19-971917-4. OCLC 227005561[357].
- Connaughton, Richard; Pimlott, David; Anderson, Duncan (1995). *The Battle for Manila*. London: Bloomsbury. ISBN 0-7475-3709-7. OCLC 260177075[358].
- Costello, John (1981). *The Pacific War*. New York: Rawson, Wade. ISBN 0-89256-206-4. OCLC 7554100[359].
- Craven, Wesley Frank; Cate, James Lea, eds. (1948). *Vol. I, Plans and Early Operations*[360]. The Army Air Forces in World War II. Chicago: University of Chicago Press. OCLC 9828710[361]. Retrieved 30 March 2006.
- Danner, Stephen A. (1993). *The Truman-MacArthur Tug of War – A Lingering Aftermath*[362]. Maxwell Air Force Base, Alabama: Air War College. OCLC 50988290[363]. Retrieved 16 May 2011.
- Dexter, David (1961). *The New Guinea Offensives*[364]. Australia in the War of 1939–1945. Series 1 – Army. Volume 6. Canberra: Australian War Memorial. OCLC 2028994[365].
- Dingman, Roger (Winter 1988–1989). "Atomic Diplomacy during the Korean War". *International Security*. Cambridge, Massachusetts: The MIT Press. **13** (3): 50–91. doi: 10.2307/2538736[366]. JSTOR 2538736[367].
- Dower, John (1999). *Embracing Defeat: Japan in the Wake of World War II*. New York: W. W. Norton & Company. ISBN 978-0-393-32027-5. OCLC 39143090[368].
- Drea, Edward J (1992). *MacArthur's ULTRA: Codebreaking and the War Against Japan, 1942–1945*. Lawrence, Kansas: University Press of Kansas. ISBN 0-7006-0504-5. OCLC 23651196[369].
- Drea, Edward; Bradsher, Greg; Hanyok, Robert; Lide, James; Petersen, Michael; Yang, Daqing (2006). *Researching Japanese War Crimes*

Records. Washington, D.C.: National Archives and Records Administration. ISBN 1-880875-28-4. OCLC 71126844[370].

- Farwell, Byron (1999). *Over There: The United States in the Great War, 1917–1918*. New York: W.W. Norton & Company. ISBN 0-393-04698-2. OCLC 39478133[371].
- Ferrell, Robert H. (2008). *The Question of MacArthur's Reputation: Côte-de-Châttillon October 14–16, 1918*. Columbia, Missouri: University of Missouri Press. ISBN 978-0-8262-1830-8. OCLC 227919803[372].
- Foster, Frank C. (2011). *United States Army Medals, Badges and Insignia*. Fountain Inn, South Carolina: Medals of America Press,. ISBN 978-1-884452-67-3. OCLC 747618459[373].
- Frank, Richard B. (2007). *MacArthur*. Great Generals Series. New York: Palgrave Macmillan. ISBN 978-1-4039-7658-1. OCLC 126872347[374].
- Gailey, Harry A. (2004). *MacArthur's Victory: The War in New Guinea, 1943–1944*. New York: Presidio Press. ISBN 0-345-46386-2. OCLC 54966430[375].
- Gold, Hal (1996). *Unit 731 Testimony*. Boston: Tuttle. ISBN 0-8048-3565-9. OCLC 57440210[376].
- Goulden, Joseph C. (1982). *Korea, The Untold Story of the War*. McGraw-Hill. ISBN 0-07-023580-5. OCLC 7998103[377].
- Halberstam, David (2007). *The Coldest Winter: America and the Korean War*. New York: Hyperion. ISBN 1-4013-0052-9. OCLC 137324872[378].
- Hayes, Grace P. (1982). *The History of the Joint Chiefs of Staff in World War II: The War Against Japan*. Annapolis: United States Naval Institute. ISBN 0-87021-269-9. OCLC 7795125[379].
- Hetherington, John (1973). *Blamey, Controversial Soldier: a Biography of Field Marshal Sir Thomas Blamey*. Canberra: Australian War Memorial. ISBN 0-9592043-0-X. OCLC 2025093[380].
- Imparato, E. T. (2000). *General MacArthur: Speeches and Reports 1908–1964*. Paducah, Kentucky: Turner Pub. ISBN 1-56311-589-1. OCLC 45603650[381].
- James, D. Clayton (1970). *Volume 1, 1880–1941*. The Years of MacArthur. Boston: Houghton Mifflin. ISBN 0-395-10948-5. OCLC 60070186[382].
- —— (1975). *Volume 2, 1941–1945*. The Years of MacArthur. Boston: Houghton Mifflin. ISBN 0-395-20446-1. OCLC 12591897[383].
- —— (1985). *Volume 3, Triumph and Disaster 1945–1964*. The Years of MacArthur. Boston: Houghton Mifflin. ISBN 0-395-36004-8. OCLC 36211311[384].
- Kenney, George C. (1949). *General Kenney Reports: A Personal History of the Pacific War*[385]. New York: Duell, Sloan and Pearce. ISBN 0-

912799-44-7. OCLC 16466573[386]. Retrieved 20 February 2009.

- Leary, William M., ed. (2001). *MacArthur and the American Century: A Reader*. Lincoln: University of Nebraska Press. ISBN 0-8032-2930-5. OCLC 44420468[387].
- Long, Gavin Merrick (1969). *MacArthur as Military Commander*. London: Batsford. ISBN 978-0-938289-14-2. OCLC 464094918[388].
- Lowe, Peter (July 1990). "An Ally and a Recalcitrant General: Great Britain, Douglas MacArthur and the Korean War, 1950–1". *The English Historical Review*. Oxford: Oxford University Press. **105** (416): 624–653. doi: 10.1093/ehr/cv.ccccxvi.624[389]. JSTOR 570755[390].
- Lucas, John A. (1994). "USOC President Douglas MacArthur and His Olympic Moment, 1927–1928"[391] (PDF). *Olympika: the International Journal of Olympic Studies*. **III**: 111–115.
- Luvaas, Jay (1972). *Dear Miss Em: General Eichelberger's war in the Pacific, 1942–1945*. Westport, Connecticut: Greenwood Press. ISBN 0-8371-6278-5. OCLC 415330[392].
- MacArthur, Douglas (1964). *Reminiscences of General of the Army Douglas MacArthur*. Annapolis: Bluejacket Books. ISBN 1-55750-483-0. OCLC 220661276[393].
- Manchester, William (1978). *American Caesar: Douglas MacArthur 1880–1964*. Boston: Little, Brown. ISBN 0-440-30424-5. OCLC 3844481[394].
- Marshall, Charles Burton (1989). "Interview Transcript of Oral History Interview with Charles Burton Marshall by Niel M. Johnson in Washington, DC, June 21 and 23, 1989"[395]. Harry S. Truman Library and Museum. Retrieved 27 October 2015.
- McCarthy, Dudley (1959). *South-West Pacific Area – First Year*[396]. Australia in the War of 1939–1945. Series 1 – Army. Volume 5. Canberra: Australian War Memorial. OCLC 3134247[397].
- Meilinger, Phillip S. (1989). *Hoyt S. Vandenberg, the Life of a General*. Bloomington, Indiana: Indiana University Press. ISBN 0-253-32862-4. OCLC 18164655[398].
- Milner, Samuel (1957). *Victory in Papua*[399]. United States Army in World War II. Washington, D.C.: United States Department of the Army. ISBN 1-4102-0386-7. OCLC 1260772[400]. Retrieved 13 March 2010.
- Morison, Samuel Eliot (1950). *Breaking the Bismarcks Barrier: 22 July 1942–1 May 1944*. History of United States Naval Operations in World War II. Boston: Little, Brown and Company. ISBN 0-7858-1307-1. OCLC 10310299[401].
- Morton, Louis (1953). *The Fall of the Philippines*[402] (PDF). United States Army in World War II. Washington, D.C.: United States Department of the Army. ISBN 1-4102-1696-9. OCLC 29293689[403]. Retrieved 17

October 2011.

- Mossman, B.; Stark, M. W. (1991). *The Last Salute: Civil and Military Funeral, 1921–1969,*[404]. Washington, D.C.: United States Department of the Army. Retrieved 11 March 2010.*
- Murray, Williamson; Millet, Alan (2001). *A War To Be Won: Fighting the Second World War*. Cambridge: Harvard University Press. ISBN 9780674006805.
- Nitze, Paul H.; Smith, Ann M.; Rearden, Steven L. (1989). *From Hiroshima to Glasnost – At the Center of Decision – A Memoir*. New York: Grove Weidenfeld. ISBN 1-55584-110-4. OCLC 19629673[405].
- Pearlman, Michael D. (2008). *Truman & MacArthur: Policy, Politics, and the Hunger for Honor and Renown*. Bloomington: Indiana University Press. ISBN 0-253-35066-2. OCLC 159919446[406].
- Perret, Geoffrey (1996). *Old Soldiers Never Die: The Life of Douglas MacArthur*. New York: Random House. ISBN 0-679-42882-8. OCLC 32396366[407].
- Petillo, Carol M. (February 1979). *Douglas MacArthur and Manuel Quezon: A Note on an Imperial Bond*. *Pacific Historical Review*. Volume 48. University of California Press. pp. 107–117. JSTOR 3638940[408].
- —— (1981). *MacArthur: The Philippine Years*. Bloomington: Indiana University Press. ISBN 0-253-11248-6. OCLC 7815453[409].
- Pettinger, Matthew R. (2003). *Held to a Higher Standard: The Downfall of Admiral Kimmel*[410]. Fort Leavenworth, Kansas: US Army Command and General Staff College. OCLC 465214958[411]. Retrieved 22 May 2011.
- Rhoades, Weldon E. (1987). *Flying MacArthur to Victory*. College Station, Texas: Texas A & M University Press. ISBN 0-585-17430-X. OCLC 44965807[412].
- Rogers, Paul P. (1990). *The Good Years: MacArthur and Sutherland*. New York: Praeger Publishers. ISBN 0-275-92918-3. OCLC 20452987[413].
- —— (1991). *The Bitter Years: MacArthur and Sutherland*. New York: Praeger Publishers. ISBN 0-275-92919-1. OCLC 21523648[414].
- Schaller, Michael (1985). *The American Occupation of Japan: The Origins of the Cold War in Asia*. New York: Oxford University Press. ISBN 0-19-503626-3. OCLC 11971554[415].
- Schaller, Michael (1989). *Douglas MacArthur The Far Eastern General*. New York: Oxford University Press. ISBN 0-19-503886-X. OCLC 11971554[415].
- Schnabel, James F (1972). *Policy and Direction: the First Year*[416]. United States Army in the Korean War. Washington, D.C.: US Government Printing Office. OCLC 595249[417]. Retrieved 17 May 2011.

- Schonberger, Howard (Spring 1974). "The General and the Presidency: Douglas MacArthur and the Election of 1948". *The Wisconsin Magazine of History*. Madison, Wisconsin: Wisconsin Historical Society. **57** (3): 201–219. doi: 10.2307/1988372[354]. JSTOR 4634887[418].
- Senate Committees on Armed Services and Foreign Relations, Hearings, 82d Congress, 1st session (1951). *Military Situation in the Far East*[419]. Washington, D.C.: US Government Printing Office. OCLC 4956423[420]. Retrieved 11 September 2011.
- Spanier, John W. (1959). *The Truman-MacArthur Controversy and the Korean War*. Cambridge, Massachusetts: Belknap Press of Harvard University Press. ISBN 0674366026. OCLC 412555[421].
- Stanton, Shelby L. (1989). *America's Tenth Legion*. Novato, California: Presidio. ISBN 0-89141-258-1. OCLC 19921899[422].
- Taaffe, Stephen (1998). *MacArthur's Jungle War: The 1944 New Guinea Campaign*. Lawrence, Kansas: University Press of Kansas. ISBN 0-7006-0870-2. OCLC 37107216[423].
- Thompson, James (2006). *Complete Guide to United States Marine Corps Medals, Badges and Insignia: World War II to Present*. Fountain Inn, South Carolina: MOA Press. ISBN 1-884452-43-4. OCLC 131299310[424].
- Torricelli, Robert G.; Carroll, Andrew; Goodwin, Doris Kearns (2008). *In Our Own Words: Extraordinary Speeches of the American Century*. Washington Square Press. ISBN 978-0-7434-1052-6. OCLC 45144217[425].
- Valley, David J. (2000). *Gaijin Shogun: General Douglas MacArthur, Stepfather of Postwar Japan*. Sektor Company. ISBN 0-9678175-2-8. OCLC 45586737[426].
- Vierk, Valerie Lee (2005). *Gold Stars and Purple Hearts: the War Dead of the Ravenna, Nebraska Area*. Bloomington, Indiana: AuthorHouse. ISBN 1-4208-7607-4. OCLC 70700519[427].
- Weinberg, Gerhard L. (2004). *A World at Arms: A Global History of World War II*. Cambridge University Press. ISBN 978-0-521-61826-7. OCLC 45586737[426].
- Willoughby, Charles A., ed. (1966). *Japanese Operations in the Southwest Pacific Area Volume II – Part I*[428]. Reports of General MacArthur. Washington, D.C.: United States Government Printing Office. OCLC 482111659[429]. CMH Pub 13-1. Retrieved 10 February 2009.

Further reading

<templatestyles src="Template:Refbegin/styles.css" />

- Barbey, Daniel E. (1969). *MacArthur's Amphibious Navy: Seventh Amphibious Force Operations, 1943–1945*. Annapolis, Maryland: United States Naval Institute. OCLC 52066[430].
- Bartsch, William H. (2003). *8 December 1941: MacArthur's Pearl Harbor*. College Station, Texas: Texas A&M University Press. ISBN 1-58544-246-1. OCLC 50920708[431].
- Bix, Herbert P. (2000). *Hirohito and the Making of Modern Japan*. New York: HarperCollins. ISBN 0-06-019314-X. OCLC 43031388[432].
- Davis, Henry Blaine, Jr. (1998). *Generals in Khaki*. Raleigh, North Carolina: Pentland Press, Inc. ISBN 978-1-57197-088-6. OCLC 40298151[433].
- Duffy, Bernard K; Carpenter, Ronald H. (1997). *Douglas MacArthur: Warrior as Wordsmith*. Westport, Connecticut: Greenwood Press. ISBN 0-313-29148-9. OCLC 34117548[434].
- Leary, William M., ed. (1988). *We Shall Return!: MacArthur's Commanders and the Defeat of Japan, 1942–1945*. Lexington, Kentucky: University Press of Kentucky. ISBN 978-0-8131-9105-8. OCLC 17483104[435].
- Lowitt, Richard (1967). *The Truman-MacArthur Controversy*. Chicago: Rand McNally. ISBN 978-0-528-66344-4. OCLC 712199[436].
- Lutz, David W. (January 2000). "The Exercise of Military Judgment: A Philosophical Investigation of The Virtues And Vices of General Douglas MacArthur". *Journal of Power and Ethics* (1).
- Masuda, Hiroshi (2012). *MacArthur in Asia: The General and His Staff in the Philippines, Japan, and Korea*. Ithaca, New York: Cornell University Press. ISBN 978-0-8014-4939-0. OCLC 780415694[437].
- Rasor, Eugene L. (1994). *General Douglas MacArthur, 1880–1964: Historiography and Annotated Bibliography*. Westport, Connecticut: Greenwood Press. ISBN 978-0-313-28873-9. OCLC 29428597[438].
- Schaller, Michael (1964). *Douglas MacArthur: The Far Eastern General*. New York: Oxford University Press. ISBN 0-7351-0354-2. OCLC 18325485[439].
- Schonberger, Howard B. (1989). *Aftermath of War: Americans and the Remaking of Japan, 1945–1952*. American Diplomatic History. Kent, Ohio: Kent State University Press. ISBN 978-0-87338-382-0. OCLC 18557205[440].
- Sodei, Rinjirō (1964). *Dear General MacArthur: Letters from the Japanese During the American Occupation*. Lanham, Maryland: Rowman & Littlefield Publishers. ISBN 0-7425-1115-4. OCLC 47177004[441].

- Wainstock, Dennis D. (1999). *Truman, MacArthur, and the Korean War*. Contributions in Military Studies. Westport, Connecticut: Greenwood Press. ISBN 978-0-313-30837-6. OCLC 261176470[442].
- Weintraub, Stanley (2000). *MacArthur's War: Korea and the Undoing of an American Hero*. New York: Free Press. ISBN 0-684-83419-7. OCLC 41548333[443].
- Wolfe, Robert (1984). *Americans as Proconsuls: United States Military Government in Germany and Japan, 1944–1952*. Carbondale, Illinois: Southern Illinois University Press. ISBN 978-0-8093-1115-6. OCLC 9465314[444].

External links

<templatestyles src="Template:Refbegin/styles.css" />

- Works by or about Douglas MacArthur[445] at Internet Archive
- "Douglas MacArthur"[446]. *Hall of Valor*. Military Times.
- "The MacArthur Memorial"[447].
- "The MacArthur Museum of Arkansas Military History"[448]. City of Little Rock.
- "Obituary: Commander of Armies That Turned Back Japan Led a Brigade in World War I"[449]. *New York Times*. 6 April 1964.
- "MacArthur"[450]. PBS. Archived from the original[451] on 18 February 2017.
- "Douglas MacArthur"[452]. History.
- The short film *Big Picture: The Douglas MacArthur Story*[453] is available for free download at the Internet Archive
- Truman Fires MacArthur, Aftermath: Original Letters[454]
- Senate joint resolution to authorize the appointment of General of the Army Douglas MacArthur as General of the Armies of the United States
- Douglas MacArthur[455] on IMDb
- FBI file on General Douglas MacArthur[456] at vault.fbi.gov
- "MacArthur Museum Brisbane"[457]. AMP Building, Cnr of Queen and Edward Sts, Brisbane, Queensland, Australia.
- Appearances[458] on C-SPAN
- Newspaper clippings about Douglas MacArthur[459] in the 20th Century Press Archives of the German National Library of Economics (ZBW)

Military offices		
Preceded by **Samuel Escue Tillman**	**Superintendent of the United States Military Academy** 1919–1922	Succeeded by **Fred Winchester Sladen**
Preceded by **Charles P. Summerall**	**Chief of Staff of the United States Army** 1930–1935	Succeeded by **Malin Craig**
New office	**Supreme Commander for the Allied Powers** 1945–1951	Succeeded by **Matthew Ridgway**
Party political offices		
Preceded by **Dwight H. Green**	**Keynote Speaker of the Republican National Convention** 1952	Succeeded by **Arthur B. Langlie**
Awards		
Preceded by **Dwight D. Eisenhower**	**Recipient of the Sylvanus Thayer Award** 1962	Succeeded by **John J. McCloy**
Honorary titles		
Preceded by **John F. Kennedy**	**Persons who have lain in state or honor in the United States Capitol rotunda** 1964	Succeeded by **Herbert Hoover**

Service summary of Douglas MacArthur

Douglas MacArthur, United States Army General began his career in 1899, served in three major military conflicts and held the highest military office of the United States and of the Philippines during that service.

Summary of service

West Point

- June 13, 1899 – appointed as a Cadet at the United States Military Academy, West Point, New York.
- 1900: Is the victim of hazing and becomes involved in a serious scandal where one Cadet is left dead by upperclassman abuse. During the investigation he implicates only cadets who were already expelled from West Point or had previously confessed.
- June 1903 – Graduates first in his class, commissioned as a Second Lieutenant in the Corps of Engineers

Early career

- June 1903: Serves with the 33rd Battalion of Engineers in the Philippine Islands.
- 1904: Assigned to the California Debris Commission.
- April 1904: Promoted to First Lieutenant, becomes acting Chief Engineering Officer for the Army Pacific Division based in San Francisco, California
- October 1904: Reports to Tokyo, Japan to serve as an aide to his father (Major General Arthur MacArthur, Jr.) in the Far East
- December 1906: Serves as aide-de-camp to President Theodore Roosevelt
- August 1907: Attends the "Engineering School of Application" in Washington, D.C.
- February 1908: Assigned as the Officer-in-Charge (OIC), Improvements Commission, Milwaukee, Wisconsin
- April 1908: Appointed as Commanding Officer, Company K, 3rd Battalion of Engineers. Later that year becomes an instructor at the Mounted Service School, Fort Riley, Kansas
- April 1909: Becomes Quartermaster for the 3rd Battalion of Engineers
- February 1911: Promoted to Captain and serves as the Officer-in-Charge of the Engineering Depot at Fort Leavenworth, Kansas
- November 1912: Assigned to the General Staff Corps, for duty as a Member and Recorder of the Board of Engineering Troops
- April 1913: Appointed as Superintendent of the State, War, and Navy Building in Washington, D.C. as a member of the Army General Staff
- April 1914: Becomes the Assistant Engineering Officer of the military expedition to Veracruz, Mexico
- December 1915: Promoted to Major, serves as an Engineering Officer on the Army General Staff
- August 1917: Advanced to the temporary rank of Colonel in the National Army. Reports to Camp Mills, Long Island, New York to begin forming the 42nd Division.

World War I

- 1917 – 1918: Becomes Chief of Staff of the 42nd Division and is credited with naming it the "Rainbow Division". Joins the American Expeditionary Force bound for France. Departs U.S. for France in November 1917.
- June 1918: Appointed a Brigadier General in the National Army and in August is appointed as Commander of the 84th Infantry Brigade. Briefly commands the 42nd Division from 10 to 22 November 1918.

- 1918 – 1919: Receives two Distinguished Service Crosses and seven Silver Star Citations (later converted to Silver Stars) for battlefield leadership and bravery and also is wounded in action and gassed by the enemy. Was known for personally leading troops into battle, often without a weapon of his own. Begins to develop a negative relationship with General of the Armies John Pershing, after feeling that Pershing is wasting the lives of his troops with bad military tactics.
- May 1919: Returns to the United States as a hero, but is distraught over the lack of recognition his Rainbow Division receives for actions in France.

Inter-war years

- June 12, 1919: Becomes the Superintendent of the United States Military Academy, West Point.[460]
- January 20, 1920: Appointed as a brigadier general in the Regular Army. Is one of the few officers who retain their wartime rank. Receives a negative evaluation report from Pershing, now Chief of Staff, who ranks Macarthur 38 out of 45 generals and states that MacArthur has an "exalted view of himself and should remain in his present grade for several years".
- November 1, 1922: Becomes Commanding General, District of Manila, in the Philippines.
- June 29, 1923: While still serving as District of Manila Commander, also becomes commander of the 23rd Infantry Brigade.
- November 18, 1924: Assigned as commander of the Philippine Division.
- January 17, 1925: Promoted to major general, becoming the youngest two-star general in the U.S. Army. Returns to the United States to become a corps commander.
- May 1, 1925: Assigned as 4th Corps Area Commander, encompassing the southeastern states with headquarters in Atlanta. Quickly reassigned as local residents did not welcome MacArthur because his father was a Union officer during the Civil War.
- August 1, 1925 – September 3, 1928: Serves as 3rd Corps Area Commander, with headquarters in Baltimore, Maryland.
- Summer 1928: Leads the United States Olympic Team to Amsterdam.
- October 1, 1928: Assigned as the Commanding General of the Philippine Department, with headquarters in Manila.
- October 2, 1930: Becomes the commander of the Ninth Corps Area with headquarters at the Presidio of San Francisco, California.
- November 21, 1930: Appointed by President Hoover as Chief of Staff of the United States Army and promoted to the rank of general on the same date.

- June 1932: Presides over the dispersal of the "Bonus Army", deemed a low point of his tenure as Army Chief of Staff.
- October 1, 1935: Completes his tour as Chief of Staff and declines retirement from the Army. Per Army regulations, reverts to his permanent rank of Major General and becomes the Chief Military Advisor to the Commonwealth Government of the Philippines.
- April 30, 1937: marries Jean Faircloth in New York City.
- December 31, 1937: Retires from the Army at his own request. Placed on the retired list as a four-star general.
- 1937 – 1941: Civilian adviser to the Philippine Government on military matters. Is appointed a Field Marshal in the Philippine Army, the only American officer in history accorded with that rank. Begins wearing the "scrambled eggs" cap often associated with him.
- February 21, 1938: Son Arthur MacArthur IV is born.

World War II

- July 26, 1941: Recalled to active service in the United States Army as a Major General.
- July 27, 1941: Appointed Lieutenant General in the Army of the United States and becomes Commanding General of USAFFE (United States Army Forces in the Far East).
- December 8, 1941: Japanese invade the Philippines.
- December 18, 1941: promoted to General in the Army of the United States.
- December 1941–May 1942; Allied forces retreat to Bataan and Corregidor
- February–March 1942: Roosevelt orders MacArthur to leave the Philippines and base in himself in Australia; on March 20, in Terowie, South Australia, MacArthur promises, "I came out of Bataan and I shall return."
- May 1942: MacArthur is appointed Supreme Allied Commander, South West Pacific Area. Australian Prime Minister John Curtin gives MacArthur control of the Australian military, which commences the New Guinea campaign.
- 1943: MacArthur implements Operation Cartwheel, the Joint Chiefs of Staff plan to isolate the major Japanese base at Rabaul.
- 1943 – 1944: argues with the Joint Chiefs of Staff regarding reconquest of the Philippine Islands. Chiefs propose bypass; MacArthur appeals to President Roosevelt.
- October 20, 1944: MacArthur fulfills his promise to return to the Philippines. U.S. forces landed at Leyte and began reconquest of Philippines.
- December 18, 1944: Promoted to the newly created rank of General of the Army becoming second highest ranking active duty officer of the U.S. Army, second only to George Marshall.

- 1944 – 1945: Due to logistics issues the Joint Chiefs decided to invade the Philippine Islands. MacArthur again must fight to convince his superiors to invade the entire Philippine Islands, whereas initial plans call for only an invasion of the south. The Joint Chiefs at last agreed that MacArthur is to invade the Philippine Islands at Leyte Gulf and strike toward Manila.
- February 5, 1945: Forces under MacArthur's command liberate Manila.
- Summer 1945: in Manila to plan invasions of Japan in October, 1945. Is stunned by the news of the use of the atomic bomb, and is quoted as saying that "this apparatus will make men like me obsolete".
- September 2, 1945: Presided over the Japanese surrender ceremony and is appointed military governor of Japanese home islands. Threatens the Soviet Union with armed conflict should Red Army soldiers attempt to occupy any part of Japan.

Occupation of Japan

- December 15, 1945: Orders the end of Shinto as the state religion of Japan.
- 1945 – 1948: Begins sweeping reforms, drafts a new constitution for Japan, and puts an end to centuries of Emperor god-worship.

Korean War

- June 25, 1950: Invasion by North Korea into South Korea.
- July 8, 1950: Named Commander-in-Chief of all United Nations forces in Korea.
- July 31, 1950: Travels to Taiwan and conducts diplomacy with Generalissimo Chiang Kai-shek.
- September 15, 1950: Leads UN forces at the Battle of Inchon, seen as one of the greatest military maneuvers in history.
- October 15, 1950: Meets with President Truman on Wake Island after heavy disagreements develop regarding the conduct of the Korean War. When meeting Truman, it is very noticeable that MacArthur does not salute his Commander-in-Chief but rather offers a handshake. Truman awards MacArthur a fourth oak leaf cluster on his Distinguished Service Medal.
- November – December 1950: With China committed to all-out war against the US on the Korean peninsula, MacArthur advocates for the same in return against China but is prohibited. He is outraged when military leaders in Washington restrict the war to only the Korean theater, meaning that he cannot bomb even the bridges of the Yalu river over which Chinese troops, supplies, and material are streaming across. He

is further restricted from bombing their bases in Manchuria. MacArthur expressed his outrage later, saying that "The order not to bomb the Yalu bridges was the most indefensible and ill-conceived decision ever forced on a field commander in our nation's history."

- April 11, 1951: After several public criticisms of White House policy in Korea, which were seen as undercutting the Commander-in-Chief's position, Harry Truman removes MacArthur from command and orders him to return to the United States. Some suggest Truman may have exchanged MacArthur for a sound nuclear policy in Korea since he did not trust "Brass Hat MacArthur" with nuclear weapons. Some disagree with this, however, since (as David Horowitz noted in *The Free World Colossus*) MacArthur later came out against Truman's use of the bomb against Japan and there seems to be no concrete evidence of a major change in his views.
- April 19, 1951: At a farewell address before the United States Congress, MacArthur gives his famous "Old Soldiers Never Die" speech[461].
- May 1951: Retires a second time from the U.S. Army, but is listed as permanently on active duty due to the regulations regarding those who hold the rank of General of the Army. For administrative reasons, he is assigned *in absentee* to the office of the Army Chief of Staff.

Later life

- 1952: Allows name to be placed on primary ballots for Republican nomination, but does not campaign or announce as a candidate. Senator Robert Taft promises supporters to name MacArthur as candidate for Vice President, but Taft loses nomination to Eisenhower.
- 1955: Is considered for promotion to the rank of General of the Armies. The promotion does not take place, various difficulties having arisen.
- May 12, 1962: Gives famous *Duty, Honor, Country* speech at West Point upon accepting the Sylvanus Thayer Award granted by the West Point Association of Graduates.
- Active in U.S. Olympic affairs.
- April 5, 1964: Douglas MacArthur dies of liver and kidney failure following gallbladder surgery at Walter Reed Army Medical Center in Washington, D.C.

Dates of rank

Insignia	Rank	Component	Date
None	Cadet	United States Military Academy	June 13, 1899
No pin insignia in 1903	Second Lieutenant, Engineers	Regular Army	June 11, 1903
	First Lieutenant, Engineers	Regular Army	April 23, 1904
	Captain, Engineers	Regular Army	February 27, 1911
	Major, Engineers	Regular Army	December 11, 1915
	Colonel, Infantry	National Army	August 11, 1917 (Date of rank was August 5, 1917.)
	Brigadier General	National Army	July 11, 1918. (Date of rank was June 26, 1918.)
	Brigadier General	Regular Army	February 28, 1920 (Date of rank was January 20, 1920.)
	Major General	Regular Army	January 17, 1925
	General	Temporary	November 21, 1930
	Reverted to Major General	Regular Army	October 1, 1935
	General	Retired list	January 1, 1938
	Major General	Regular Army	July 26, 1941 (Recalled to active duty.)
	Lieutenant General	Army of the United States	July 27, 1941
	General	Army of the United States	December 22, 1941 (With date of rank September 16, 1936.)
	General of the Army	Army of the United States	December 18, 1944
	General of the Army	Regular Army	March 23, 1946

462

In 1955, legislation was in the early stages of consideration by the United States Congress which would have authorized the President of the United States to promote Douglas MacArthur to the rank of General of the Armies. A similar measure had also been proposed unsuccessfully by Stuart Symington in 1945. However, because of several complications which would arise if such a promotion were to take place, the bill was withdrawn.

Awards and decorations

During his military career, General MacArthur was awarded the following decorations from the United States and other allied nations. The list below is of those medals worn on a military uniform, and does not include commemorative medals, unofficial decorations, and non-portable awards.

Badges

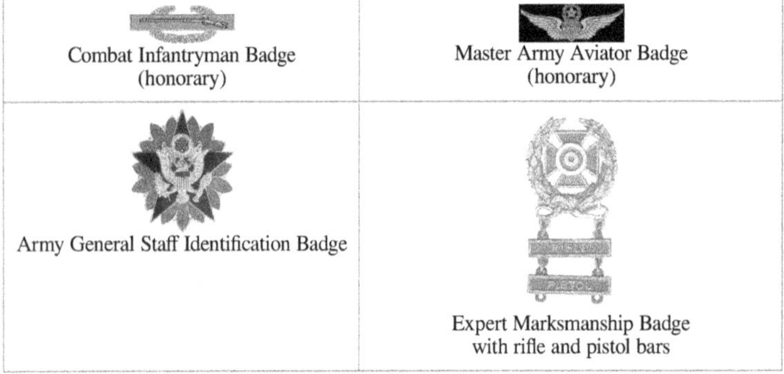

Combat Infantryman Badge (honorary)

Master Army Aviator Badge (honorary)

Army General Staff Identification Badge

Expert Marksmanship Badge with rifle and pistol bars

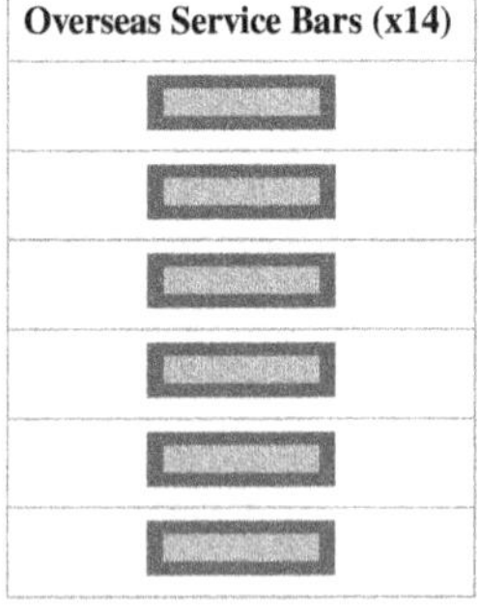

Overseas Service Bars (x14)

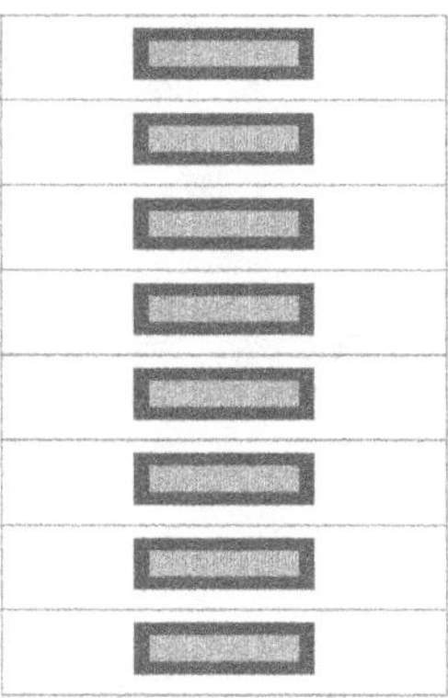

Award ribbons

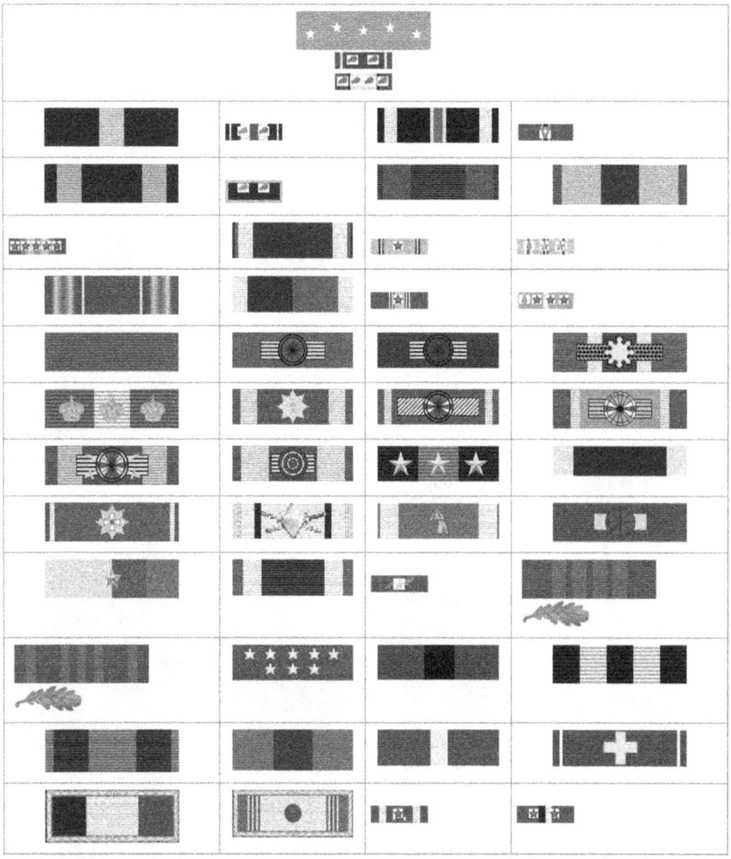

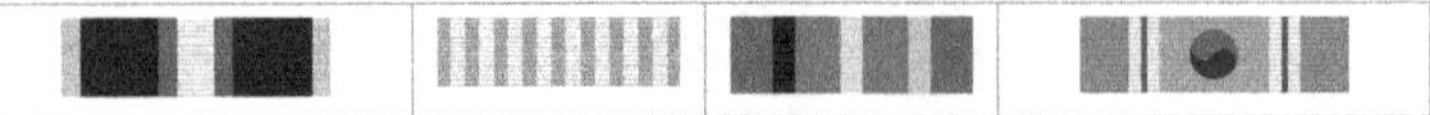

Award names

Medal of Honor	Distinguished Service Cross with two oak leaf clusters	Army Distinguished Service Medal with four oak leaf clusters

Navy Distinguished Service Medal	Silver Star with six oak leaf clusters	Distinguished Flying Cross	Bronze Star with "V" device
Air Medal	Presidential Unit Citation with six oak leaf clusters	Philippine Campaign Medal	Mexican Service Medal
World War I Victory Medal with five battle clasps	Army of Occupation of Germany Medal	American Defense Service Medal with "Foreign Service" clasp	Asiatic-Pacific Campaign Medal with two silver service stars & arrowhead device
World War II Victory Medal	Army of Occupation Medal with "Japan" clasp	National Defense Service Medal (posthumously eligible for bronze service star)	Korean Service Medal with three bronze service stars & arrowhead device
Knight Grand Cross of the Most Honourable Order of the Bath (Military Division)	Grand Cross of the Legion of Honour	Belgian Order of the Crown, Grand Cross	Philippine Legion of Honor Degree of Chief Commander
Grand Cordon, Order of the Crown of Italy	Czechoslovakian Military Order of the White Lion, Grand Cross	Polish Order of Polonia Restituta, Grand Cross	Grand Cross Netherlands Order of Orange-Nassau with Swords
Yugoslavian Order of the White Eagle, Grand Cross with swords	Japanese Order of the Rising Sun with Paulownia Flowers	Knight Grand Cross of Military Order of Italy	Chinese Special Grand Cordon Order of Pao Ting (Precious Tripod)
Hungarian Grand Cross of the Order of Merit (Military Division)	Grand Cross Order of Romanian Military Merit	Korean Taegeuk Cordon of the Order of Military Merit	Grand Cross of the Order of Merit "Carlos Manuel de Céspedes" (Cuba)
Ecuadorian Star of Abdon Calderon, First Class	Order of Lafayette (*Unconfirmed*)	French Croix de Guerre with palm and gilt star	French Croix de Guerre (1939-1945) with palm
Belgian Croix de Guerre with Palm	Philippine Medal of Valor	Philippine Distinguished Conduct Star	Italian War Merit Cross
Polish Virtuti Militari, V Class	Greek War Cross	Mexican Medal of Military Merit	Guatemalan Cross of Military Merit, First Class

Philippine Presidential Unit Citation	Republic of Korea Presidential Unit Citation	Philippine Defense Medal with one bronze campaign star	Philippine Liberation Medal with two bronze campaign stars
Philippine Independence Medal	United Nations Korea Medal	Pacific Star (United Kingdom)	Republic of Korea War Service Medal *(posthumous)*

Memberships

General MacArthur belonged to several military and hereditary societies including the Society of the Cincinnati (honorary member of the New York Society), Military Order of the Loyal Legion of the United States (insignia number 15,317), Sons of Union Veterans of the Civil War, Sons of the American Revolution (accepted by the Empire State Society on August 27, 1945, and assigned national membership number 65,843 and state membership number 7,723), Military Order of Foreign Wars, Military Order of the World Wars (of which he served as national commander in 1928) and the American Legion. In 1942 he received the American Legion's Distinguished Service Medal. On October 13, 1951, he was elected an honorary national president of the Society of American Legion Founders.[463]

He was also eligible for membership in the Order of Lafayette, Sons of the Revolution, Society of Colonial Wars, Order of the Indian Wars of the United States, Military Order of the Carabao, United Spanish War Veterans and the Veterans of Foreign Wars, but his membership in these organizations has not been confirmed.

On January 17, 1936, MacArthur was made a Freemason at sight by Samuel Hawthorne, Grand Master of Masons in the Philippines in a two-hour ceremony. After being raised to the degree of Master Mason, MacArthur joined Manila Lodge No.1. On October 19, 1937, he was elected Knight Commander Court of Honor, and on December 8, 1947, he was coroneted to the honorary 33rd Degree at the American Embassy in Tokyo. He was also a life member of the Nile Shrine in Seattle, Washington.

External links

- *New York Times* Obituary[464]
- General Orders No. 13, Headquarters, Department of the Army, 6 April 1964.[465]

Appendix

References

[1]MacArthur 1964, pp. 13–14.
[2]MacArthur 1964, pp. 4–5.
[3]James 1970, pp. 41–42.
[4]Manchester 1978, p. 24.
[5]James 1970, p. 23.
[6]James 1970, p. 25.
[7]MacArthur 1964, p. 15.
[8]James 1970, p. 56.
[9]MacArthur 1964, pp. 16–18.
[10]James 1970, pp. 60–61.
[11]James 1970, pp. 62–66.
[12]James 1970, p. 66.
[13]MacArthur 1964, p. 25.
[14]James 1970, pp. 69–71.
[15]James 1970, p. 79.
[16]James 1970, p. 77.
[17]Manchester 1978, pp. 60–61.
[18]James 1970, pp. 87–89.
[19]Manchester 1978, p. 65.
[20]James 1970, pp. 90–91.
[21]Manchester 1978, pp. 66–67.
[22]James 1970, pp. 95–97.
[23]James 1970, pp. 105–109.
[24]James 1970, pp. 115–120.
[25]James 1970, pp. 121–125.
[26]James 1970, p. 125.
[27]James 1970, p. 124.
[28]James 1970, pp. 125–127.
[29]James 1970, pp. 130–135.
[30]James 1970, p. 148.
[31]James 1970, p. 157.
[32]Farwell 1999, p. 296.
[33]Frank 2007, p. 7.
[34]James 1970, pp. 159–160.
[35]Manchester 1978, p. 92.
[36]MacArthur 1964, pp. 57–58.
[37]James 1970, p. 187.
[38]MacArthur 1964, p. 60.
[39]MacArthur 1964, p. 61.
[40]James 1970, p. 193.
[41]James 1970, pp. 196–197.
[42]James 1970, pp. 203–204.
[43]James 1970, pp. 213–217.
[44]Ferrell 2008, pp. 47–50.
[45]MacArthur 1964, p. 66.
[46]James 1970, p. 223.
[47]MacArthur 1964, p. 67.
[48]James 1970, pp. 227–228.
[49]MacArthur 1964, p. 68.
[50]James 1970, pp. 232–233.

[51]James 1970, pp. 239–240.
[52]James 1970, pp. 241–245.
[53]James 1970, pp. 256–259.
[54]MacArthur 1964, p. 77.
[55]Manchester 1978, p. 117.
[56]James 1970, p. 265.
[57]James 1970, p. 261.
[58]Leary 2001, p. 10.
[59]James 1970, p. 262.
[60]Leary 2001, p. 11.
[61]Leary 2001, pp. 24–25.
[62]James 1970, pp. 278–279.
[63]Leary 2001, pp. 20–21.
[64]Federal Reserve Bank of Minneapolis Community Development Project. "Consumer Price Index (estimate) 1800–" https://www.minneapolisfed.org/community/financial-and-economic-education/cpi-calculator-information/consumer-price-index-1800. Federal Reserve Bank of Minneapolis. Retrieved January 2, 2018.
[65]Leary 2001, pp. 26–27.
[66]James 1970, p. 291.
[67]Manchester 1978, pp. 130–132.
[68]James 1970, p. 320.
[69]James 1970, pp. 295–297.
[70]MacArthur 1964, p. 84.
[71]James 1970, pp. 300–305.
[72]James 1970, pp. 307–310.
[73]Rhoades 1987, p. 287.
[74]MacArthur 1964, p. 85.
[75]James 1970, pp. 322.
[76]James 1970, pp. 325–332.
[77]Lucas 1994, p. 112.
[78]James 1970, p. 329.
[79]Manchester 1978, p. 141.
[80]James 1970, pp. 340–347.
[81]Manchester 1978, p. 145.
[82]Murray & Millet 2001, pp. 181.
[83]Murray & Millet 2001, pp. 182.
[84]James 1970, pp. 357–361.
[85]James 1970, p. 367.
[86]James 1970, pp. 458–460.
[87]James 1970, pp. 389–392.
[88]James 1970, p. 397.
[89]Leary 2001, pp. 36–38.
[90]Manchester 1978, p. 156.
[91]Petillo 1981, pp. 164–166.
[92]James 1970, pp. 415–420.
[93]James 1970, pp. 376–377.
[94]James 1970, pp. 445–447.
[95]MacArthur 1964, p. 101.
[96]MacArthur 1964, pp. 102–103.
[97]Vierk 2005, p. 231.
[98]Thompson 2006, p. 72.
[99]James 1970, pp. 479–484.
[100]MacArthur 1964, p. 103.
[101]James 1970, pp. 485–486.
[102]James 1970, pp. 494–495.
[103]Petillo 1981, pp. 175–176.

[104]James 1970, p. 505.
[105]MacArthur 1964, pp. 103–105.
[106]James 1970, p. 504.
[107]MacArthur 1964, p. 106.
[108]James 1970, p. 547.
[109]James 1970, p. 513.
[110]MacArthur 1964, p. 107.
[111]James 1970, p. 525.
[112]Rogers 1990, pp. 39–40.
[113]Morton 1953, p. 19.
[114]Rogers 1990, p. 100.
[115]Morton 1953, p. 21.
[116]Weinberg 2004, p. 311.
[117]Weinberg 2004, p. 312.
[118]Morton 1953, p. 50.
[119]Morton 1953, pp. 35–37.
[120]Drea 1992, p. 11.
[121]Pettinger 2003, p. 9.
[122]Pettinger 2003, pp. 9, 56.
[123]Pettinger 2003, p. 57.
[124]Morton 1953, pp. 84–88.
[125]Morton 1953, p. 97.
[126]Weinberg 2004, p. 313.
[127]Morton 1953, p. 125.
[128]Morton 1953, p. 163.
[129]Weinberg 2004, p. 313-314.
[130]Pettinger 2003, p. 53.
[131]Morton 1953, p. 164.
[132]Rogers 1990, pp. 118–121.
[133]Rogers 1990, pp. 125–141.
[134]James 1975, pp. 65–66.
[135]James 1975, p. 68.
[136]Rogers 1990, p. 165.
[137]Petillo 1979, pp. 107–117.
[138]Halberstam 2007, p. 372.
[139]James 1975, p. 98.
[140]Morton 1953, pp. 359–360.
[141]Rogers 1990, pp. 190–192.
[142]Morton 1953, pp. 463–467.
[143]Morton 1953, p. 561.
[144]James 1975, p. 129.
[145]James 1975, pp. 129–130.
[146]James 1975, p. 132.
[147]James 1975, p. 131.
[148]Manchester 1978, p. 290.
[149]Gailey 2004, pp. 7–14.
[150]Milner 1957, pp. 18–23.
[151]Rogers 1990, p. 253.
[152]Rogers 1990, pp. 275–278.
[153]Craven & Cate 1948, pp. 417–418.
[154]James 1975, pp. 197–198.
[155]Kenney 1949, p. 26.
[156]McCarthy 1959, p. 488.
[157]James 1975, p. 80.
[158]Rogers 1990, p. 202.
[159]Milner 1957, p. 48.

[160]Rogers 1990, pp. 285–287.
[161]Drea 1992, pp. 18–19.
[162]Drea 1992, p. 26.
[163]James 1975, pp. 165–166.
[164]Rogers 1990, p. 265.
[165]Milner 1957, pp. 39–41.
[166]Milner 1957, pp. 46–48.
[167]Milner 1957, pp. 53–55.
[168]Milner 1957, pp. 77–88.
[169]McCarthy 1959, p. 225.
[170]Milner 1957, pp. 91–92.
[171]McCarthy 1959, pp. 371–372.
[172]Luvaas 1972, pp. 32–33.
[173]McCarthy 1959, p. 235.
[174]Milner 1957, p. 321.
[175]James 1975, p. 275.
[176]MacArthur 1964, p. 167.
[177]Hayes 1982, pp. 312–334.
[178]Willoughby 1966, p. 100.
[179]Casey 1959, pp. 31–33.
[180]Morison 1950, pp. 130–132.
[181]James 1975, p. 220.
[182]Dexter 1961, p. 12.
[183]James 1975, p. 327.
[184]MacArthur 1964, p. 179.
[185]James 1975, pp. 328–329.
[186]James 1975, pp. 364–365.
[187]Hayes 1982, pp. 487–490.
[188]MacArthur 1964, p. 189.
[189]Willoughby 1966, pp. 137–141.
[190]Weinberg 2004, p. 654.
[191]Weinberg 2004, p. 655.
[192]Weinberg 2004, p. 1084.
[193]Weinberg 2004, p. 653.
[194]Willoughby 1966, pp. 142–143.
[195]Taaffe 1998, pp. 100–103.
[196]Drea 1992, pp. 152–159.
[197]James 1975, pp. 552–556.
[198]MacArthur 1964, p. 216.
[199]MacArthur 1964, p. 228.
[200]James 1975, pp. 561–562.
[201]MacArthur 1964, pp. 222–231.
[202]MacArthur 1964, pp. 231–234.
[203]James 1975, pp. 568–569.
[204]James 1975, pp. 602–603.
[205]This law allowed only 75% of pay and allowances to the grade for those on the retired list.
[206]James 1975, pp. 604–609.
[207]Murray & Millet 2001, pp. 495.
[208]Drea 1992, p. 186.
[209]Drea 1992, p. 187.
[210]Drea 1992, pp. 180–187.
[211]James 1975, pp. 619–620.
[212]James 1975, p. 622.
[213]James 1975, p. 629.
[214]James 1975, p. 623.
[215]James 1975, pp. 632–633.

[216] Drea 1992, pp. 195–200.
[217] Rogers 1991, p. 261.
[218] James 1975, pp. 642–644.
[219] James 1975, p. 654.
[220] MacArthur 1964, p. 244.
[221] Weinberg 2004, p. 863.
[222] Weinberg 2004, p. 863-864.
[223] Murray & Millet 2001, pp. 500-501.
[224] Murray & Millet 2001, pp. 502.
[225] James 1975, pp. 737–741.
[226] James 1975, p. 749.
[227] James 1975, pp. 757–761.
[228] MacArthur 1964, p. 260.
[229] James 1975, pp. 725–726, 765–771.
[230] Weinberg 2004, pp. 872.
[231] James 1975, pp. 786–792.
[232] MacArthur 1964, p. 265.
[233] James 1975, pp. 782–783.
[234] Bix 2000, pp. 541.
[235] Bix 2000, pp. 544-545.
[236] Bix 2000, pp. 545.
[237] Bix 2000, pp. 549.
[238] Bix 2000, pp. 550-551.
[239] Bix 2000, pp. 562.
[240] Bix 2000, pp. 567.
[241] Bix 2000, pp. 568.
[242] Bix 2000, pp. 584.
[243] Bix 2000, pp. 585.
[244] MacArthur 1964, pp. 318–319.
[245] Drea et al. 2006, p. 7.
[246] Connaughton, Pimlott & Anderson 1995, pp. 72–73.
[247] Manchester 1978, p. 487.
[248] Gold 1996, p. 109.
[249] Dower 1999, p. 323.
[250] Dower 1999, pp. 321–322.
[251] James 1985, pp. 39–139.
[252] James 1985, pp. 119–139.
[253] James 1985, pp. 183–192.
[254] James 1985, pp. 174–183.
[255] Schaller 1985, p. 25.
[256] James 1985, pp. 222–224, 252–254.
[257] Schonberger 1974, p. 202.
[258] Schonberger 1974, p. 203.
[259] Schonberger 1974, pp. 203–204.
[260] Schonberger 1974, p. 205.
[261] Schonberger 1974, p. 207.
[262] Schonberger 1974, pp. 207–208.
[263] Schonberger 1974, p. 208.
[264] Schonberger 1974, p. 213.
[265] Schonberger 1974, pp. 206–207.
[266] Schonberger 1974, pp. 212, 217.
[267] Schonberger 1974, pp. 218–219.
[268] Imparato 2000, p. 165.
[269] James 1985, pp. 336–354.
[270] Valley 2000, p. xi.
[271] James 1985, p. 387.

[272]James 1985, p. 434.
[273]James 1985, p. 436.
[274]James 1985, p. 440.
[275]James 1985, pp. 433–435.
[276]James 1985, p. 451.
[277]James 1985, p. 465.
[278]James 1985, pp. 467–469.
[279]James 1985, pp. 475–483.
[280]Stanton 1989, pp. 78–80.
[281]James 1985, pp. 486–493.
[282]James 1985, p. 500.
[283]MacArthur 1964, pp. 360–363.
[284]James 1985, pp. 507–508.
[285]Manchester 1978, p. 604.
[286]MacArthur 1964, pp. 372–373.
[287]James 1985, pp. 537–538.
[288]James 1985, p. 545.
[289]James 1985, p. 559.
[290]James 1985, pp. 578–581.
[291]Schnabel 1972, p. 320.
[292]James 1985, p. 591.
[293]Anders 1988, pp. 1–2.
[294]Anders 1988, pp. 3–4.
[295]Dingman 1988, p. 72.
[296]Schnabel 1972, pp. 300–304.
[297]Schnabel 1972, pp. 310–314.
[298]Schnabel 1972, pp. 287–292.
[299]Lowe 1990, p. 636.
[300]Schnabel 1972, pp. 333–339.
[301]Schnabel 1972, pp. 354–355.
[302]Schnabel 1972, pp. 357–359.
[303]James 1985, pp. 584–589.
[304]James 1985, p. 590.
[305]Goulden 1982, pp. 476–478.
[306]Nitze, Smith & Rearden 1989, pp. 109–111.
[307]Marshall 1989, pp. 115–117.
[308]James 1985, pp. 591–597.
[309]Pearlman 2008, p. 214.
[310]James 1985, p. 594.
[311]Meilinger 1989, p. 179.
[312]James 1985, pp. 607–608.
[313]Spanier 1959, p. ix.
[314]Casey 2008, pp. 253–254.
[315]//en.wikipedia.org/w/index.php?title=Douglas_MacArthur&action=edit
[316]Pearlman 2008, pp. 246, 326.
[317]Casey 2008, p. 327.
[318]Senate Committees on Armed Services and Foreign Relations 1951, p. 3601.
[319]James 1985, p. 611.
[320]James 1985, p. 613.
[321]Torricelli, Carroll & Goodwin 2008, pp. 185–188.
[322]Schaller 1989, p. 250.
[323]Schaller 1989, p. 250-251.
[324]Schaller 1989, p. 251.
[325]James 1985, pp. 648–652.
[326]James 1985, pp. 653–655.
[327]James 1985, pp. 655–656.

[328] James 1985, pp. 661–662.
[329] Perret 1996, pp. 581–583.
[330] James 1985, pp. 684–685.
[331] James 1985, p. 687.
[332] Perret 1996, p. 585.
[333] Mossman & Stark 1991, p. 216.
[334] Mossman & Stark 1991, pp. 225–231.
[335] Mossman & Stark 1991, pp. 236–253.
[336] Mossman & Stark 1991, p. 253.
[337] Long 1969, p. 226.
[338] Frank 2007, p. 168.
[339] Long 1969, p. 227.
[340] Pearlman 2008, p. 18.
[341] Danner 1993, pp. 14–15.
[342] Frank 2007, pp. 167–174.
[343] Hetherington 1973, p. 223.
[344] Costello 1981, p. 225.
[345] Foster 2011, p. 19.
[346] Senate Joint Resolution 26, 21 January 1955
[347] //www.worldcat.org/oclc/1163286
[348] //www.worldcat.org/oclc/456989
[349] //www.worldcat.org/oclc/562005
[350] //www.worldcat.org/oclc/456849
[351] //www.worldcat.org/oclc/1307481
[352] //www.worldcat.org/oclc/1342695
[353] //www.worldcat.org/oclc/407539
[354] //doi.org/10.2307/1988372
[355] //www.jstor.org/stable/1988372
[356] //www.worldcat.org/oclc/220327009
[357] //www.worldcat.org/oclc/227005561
[358] //www.worldcat.org/oclc/260177075
[359] //www.worldcat.org/oclc/7554100
[360] http://www.ibiblio.org/hyperwar/AAF/I/index.html
[361] //www.worldcat.org/oclc/9828710
[362] http://oai.dtic.mil/oai/oai?verb=getRecord&metadataPrefix=html&identifier=ADA283283
[363] //www.worldcat.org/oclc/50988290
[364] https://www.awm.gov.au/collection/RCDIG1070205/
[365] //www.worldcat.org/oclc/2028994
[366] //doi.org/10.2307/2538736
[367] //www.jstor.org/stable/2538736
[368] //www.worldcat.org/oclc/39143090
[369] //www.worldcat.org/oclc/23651196
[370] //www.worldcat.org/oclc/71126844
[371] //www.worldcat.org/oclc/39478133
[372] //www.worldcat.org/oclc/227919803
[373] //www.worldcat.org/oclc/747618459
[374] //www.worldcat.org/oclc/126872347
[375] //www.worldcat.org/oclc/54966430
[376] //www.worldcat.org/oclc/57440210
[377] //www.worldcat.org/oclc/7998103
[378] //www.worldcat.org/oclc/137324872
[379] //www.worldcat.org/oclc/7795125
[380] //www.worldcat.org/oclc/2025093
[381] //www.worldcat.org/oclc/45603650
[382] //www.worldcat.org/oclc/60070186
[383] //www.worldcat.org/oclc/12591897

[384] //www.worldcat.org/oclc/36211311
[385] http://www.ibiblio.org/hyperwar/AAF/AAF-Kenney/index.html
[386] //www.worldcat.org/oclc/16466573
[387] //www.worldcat.org/oclc/44420468
[388] //www.worldcat.org/oclc/464094918
[389] //doi.org/10.1093/ehr/cv.ccccxvi.624
[390] //www.jstor.org/stable/570755
[391] http://www.la84foundation.org/SportsLibrary/Olympika/Olympika_1994/olympika0301i.pdf
[392] //www.worldcat.org/oclc/415330
[393] //www.worldcat.org/oclc/220661276
[394] //www.worldcat.org/oclc/3844481
[395] https://www.trumanlibrary.org/oralhist/marshall.htm
[396] https://www.awm.gov.au/collection/RCDIG1070204/
[397] //www.worldcat.org/oclc/3134247
[398] //www.worldcat.org/oclc/18164655
[399] http://www.ibiblio.org/hyperwar/USA/USA-P-Papua/index.html
[400] //www.worldcat.org/oclc/1260772
[401] //www.worldcat.org/oclc/10310299
[402] http://www.history.army.mil/html/books/005/5-2-1/CMH_Pub_5-2-1.pdf
[403] //www.worldcat.org/oclc/29293689
[404] http://www.history.army.mil//books/Last_Salute/Ch24.htm
[405] //www.worldcat.org/oclc/19629673
[406] //www.worldcat.org/oclc/159919446
[407] //www.worldcat.org/oclc/32396366
[408] //www.jstor.org/stable/3638940
[409] //www.worldcat.org/oclc/7815453
[410] http://cgsc.contentdm.oclc.org/cdm4/item_viewer.php?CISOROOT=/p4013coll2&CISOPTR=101&CISOBOX=1&REC=14
[411] //www.worldcat.org/oclc/465214958
[412] //www.worldcat.org/oclc/44965807
[413] //www.worldcat.org/oclc/20452987
[414] //www.worldcat.org/oclc/21523648
[415] //www.worldcat.org/oclc/11971554
[416] http://www.history.army.mil/books/P&D.HTM
[417] //www.worldcat.org/oclc/595249
[418] //www.jstor.org/stable/4634887
[419] http://catalog.hathitrust.org/Record/001606736
[420] //www.worldcat.org/oclc/4956423
[421] //www.worldcat.org/oclc/412555
[422] //www.worldcat.org/oclc/19921899
[423] //www.worldcat.org/oclc/37107216
[424] //www.worldcat.org/oclc/131299310
[425] //www.worldcat.org/oclc/45144217
[426] //www.worldcat.org/oclc/45586737
[427] //www.worldcat.org/oclc/70700519
[428] http://www.history.army.mil/books/wwii/MacArthur%20Reports/MacArthur%20V2%20P1/macarthurv2.htm
[429] //www.worldcat.org/oclc/482111659
[430] //www.worldcat.org/oclc/52066
[431] //www.worldcat.org/oclc/50920708
[432] //www.worldcat.org/oclc/43031388
[433] //www.worldcat.org/oclc/40298151
[434] //www.worldcat.org/oclc/34117548
[435] //www.worldcat.org/oclc/17483104
[436] //www.worldcat.org/oclc/712199
[437] //www.worldcat.org/oclc/780415694

[438]//www.worldcat.org/oclc/29428597
[439]//www.worldcat.org/oclc/18325485
[440]//www.worldcat.org/oclc/18557205
[441]//www.worldcat.org/oclc/47177004
[442]//www.worldcat.org/oclc/261176470
[443]//www.worldcat.org/oclc/41548333
[444]//www.worldcat.org/oclc/9465314
[445]https//archive.org
[446]https://valor.militarytimes.com/hero/676
[447]http://www.macarthurmemorial.org
[448]http://www.arkmilitaryheritage.com
[449]https://www.nytimes.com/learning/general/onthisday/bday/0126.html
[450]https://web.archive.org/web/20170218010521/http://www.pbs.org/wgbh/amex/macarthur/index.html
[451]https://www.pbs.org/wgbh/amex/macarthur/index.html
[452]http://www.history.com/topics/douglas-macarthur
[453]https://archive.org/details/gov.archives.arc.2569682
[454]http://www.shapell.org/manuscript.aspx?harry-truman-fires-macarthur
[455]https://www.imdb.com/name/nm0531274/
[456]https://vault.fbi.gov/General%20Douglas%20MacArthur%20
[457]https://www.mmb.org.au/
[458]https://www.c-span.org/person/?douglasmacarthur
[459]http://purl.org/pressemappe20/folder/pe/011783
[460]Cullum's Register of Graduates of the USMA. Vol. VII pg. 576.
[461]http://www.americanrhetoric.com/speeches/douglasmacarthurfarewelladdress.htm
[462]Official Register of Commissioned Officers of the United States Army, 1948. Vol. 2. pg. 2312.
[463]New York Times. October 14, 1951.
[464]https://www.nytimes.com/learning/general/onthisday/bday/0126.html
[465]https://web.archive.org/web/20131103165818/http://armypubs.army.mil/epubs/pdf/go6413.pdf

Article Sources and Contributors

The sources listed for each article provide more detailed licensing information including the copyright status, the copyright owner, and the license conditions.

Douglas MacArthur *Source:* https://en.wikipedia.org/w/index.php?oldid=851639961 *License:* Creative Commons Attribution-Share Alike 3.0 *Contributors:* 1990'sguy, A.S. Brown, AC9016, ALOHARONN, Aeonx, Agpagpagp, Alexpl, All Hallow's Wraith, Andymii, Anonymous from the 21st century, Anotherclown, Anthony22, Aprad, Apritzker, Atvelonis, BarossaV, Baumfreund-FFM, Bender235, Beyond My Ken, BreakfastJr, Btphelps, Buckshot06, Caknuck, Caracaskid, Caroca2, Cgschmidt3169, Chris the speller, Ckfasdf, Clarityfiend, Coachfortner, Colonies Chris, ControlCorV, Cornersss, Curly Turkey, DadaNeem, Daniel Case, Dawnseeker2000, Deisenbe, DennisDallas, Diannaa, DimensionQualm, Display name 99, Doug Coldwell, DragonflySixtyseven, Eggishorn, Elendil's Heir, EricSerge, EtherealGate, FrankMJohnson, Gaylencrufts, Giraffedata, Glorious Engine, Glrx, Gobodge, GoingBatty, GoodDay, GreenC, Gulumeemee, Hawkeye7, Headbomb, HeneralVicente23, Hirolovesswords, Hugo999, I dream of horses, Iamdumdum, Ian Rose, JCO312, JHobson3, Jarble, Jdaloner, Jessicapierce, JimmyJoe87, Johnpacklambert, Jon Kolbert, Jonathan Markoff, Josephus37, Jprg1966, Kablammo, Kerry Raymond, Kev519, Kguirnela, LegalTrivia, Lieutcoluseng, Lizard the Wizard, Llammakey, Location, Lumbering in thought, MACWILMSLO, Magioladitis, Magnolia677, Marcocapelle, Mark Sublette, Mceizia2, Michael Hardy, Middle 8, MiguelMunoz, Monopoly31121993, Morio, Mr Stephen, Mr. Guye, MrFrosty2, Natg 19, Nihiltres, Notthebestusername, PanchoS, PhilOSophocle, Pigsonthewing, RFD, RHodnett, Randelearcilla200, RaphaelQS, Richard Arthur Norton (1958-), Richard Weil, Roy Jaruk, Ruedetocqueville, Saint Invective, Ser Amantio di Nicolao, Sleeping is fun, Sodacan, Solomonfromfinland, Spartan7W, Spellcast, Staszek Lem, Steve03Mills, SteveMiamiBeach, Sunuraju, Swood100, TAnthony, Tassedethe, The Gnome, The most effectual Bob Cat, Thenextprez, Therequiembellishere, Thewellman, Thorkall, Thunderbuster, Tigerdude9, Toiredundemoshunal, Tokuburai, Trappist the monk, Trekphiler, Tupelo the typo fixer, Vwanweb, Vybr8, WOSlinker, Wbm1058, Wikid77, Winged Brick, Winslowl, WinterSpw, Wwwalker, Ylee, Zedshort, Zwerubae 1

Service summary of Douglas MacArthur *Source:* https://en.wikipedia.org/w/index.php?oldid=847026195 *License:* Creative Commons Attribution-Share Alike 3.0 *Contributors:* Aec444411, Arjayay, Aumnamahashiva, AusTerrapin, Awotter, BD2412, Botpankonin, Certes, Chris the speller, Chris troutman, Claudevsq, ClueBot NG, Colonies Chris, CommonsDelinker, Dcirovic, Djharrity, Drmies, EHDI5YS, EricSerge, EuroCarGT, Haus, Hawkeye7, I dream of horses, Illegitimate Barrister, Ipankonin, Jdaloner, Jmgould, Jmgould39, Josve05a, KConWiki, Kirbanzo, Kumioko (renamed), MarkFilipak, MrDolomite, Nemesys83, OCNative, OberRanks, PrimeHunter, Producercunningham, Rcarter555, Rich Farmbrough, RightCowLeftCoast, SGT141, Sionus, Stemonitis, Thewolfchild, Timmyshin, Trappist the monk, Trout71, William von Zehle, Woohookitty, Xdamr, YahwehSaves, Yintan, 177 anonymous edits 63

Image Sources, Licenses and Contributors

The sources listed for each image provide more detailed licensing information including the copyright status, the copyright owner, and the license conditions.

Image *Source:* https://en.wikipedia.org/w/index.php?title=File:Padlock-silver.svg *Contributors:* AzaToth, BotMultichill, BotMultichillT, Gurch, Jarekt, Kallerna, Multichill, Perhelion, Rd232, Riana, Sarang, Siebrand, Steinsplitter, 4 anonymous edits ... 1
Image *Source:* https://en.wikipedia.org/w/index.php?title=File:Cscr-featured.svg *License:* GNU Lesser General Public License *Contributors:* Anomie ... 1
Image *Source:* https://en.wikipedia.org/w/index.php?title=File:MacArthur_Manila.jpg *License:* Public Domain *Contributors:* Photographer not credited. ... 1
Image *Source:* https://en.wikipedia.org/w/index.php?title=File:Flag_of_the_United_States_(1912-1959).svg *License:* Public Domain *Contributors:* Created by jacobolus using Adobe Illustrator. ... 1
Image *Source:* https://en.wikipedia.org/w/index.php?title=File:Flag_of_the_Philippines_(navy_blue).svg *License:* Creative Commons Attribution-Sharealike 2.5 *Contributors:* Alkari, Billinghurst, FakirNL, FreshCorp619, Jeenim, Kurrop, Ljmajer, Lokal Profil, MGA73bot2, Mattes, Patstuart, SiBr4, Tcfc2349, User 50, 2 anonymous edits ... 1
Image *Source:* https://en.wikipedia.org/w/index.php?title=File:Flag_of_the_United_States_Army_(official_proportions).svg *License:* Public Domain *Contributors:* United States Army ... 1
Image *Source:* https://en.wikipedia.org/w/index.php?title=File:Flag_of_the_Philippine_Army.svg *Contributors:* User:Sodacan ... 1
Image *Source:* https://en.wikipedia.org/w/index.php?title=File:US-O11_insignia.svg *License:* Public Domain *Contributors:* Ipankonin ... 1
Image *Source:* https://en.wikipedia.org/w/index.php?title=File:DMacarthur_Signature.svg *License:* Public Domain *Contributors:* Connormah, Douglas MacArthur ... 2
Figure 1 *Source:* https://en.wikipedia.org/w/index.php?title=File:View_copy.jpg *License:* Public Domain *Contributors:* Hawkeye7, Pelegius ... 4
Figure 2 *Source:* https://en.wikipedia.org/w/index.php?title=File:Douglas_MacArthur,_Army_photo_portrait_seated,_France_1918.JPEG *License:* Public Domain *Contributors:* LT. RALPH ESTEP ... 8
Figure 3 *Source:* https://en.wikipedia.org/w/index.php?title=File:General_Pershing_decorates_General_MacArthur_with_the_Distinguished_Service_Cross.jpg *License:* Public Domain *Contributors:* US Army ... 10
Figure 4 *Source:* https://en.wikipedia.org/w/index.php?title=File:Douglas_MacArthur_as_USMA_Superintendent.jpg *License:* Public Domain *Contributors:* Ahodges7, Artix Kreiger, Concord, Docu, OgreBot 2, SecretName101, Sophus Bie ... 12
Figure 5 *Source:* https://en.wikipedia.org/w/index.php?title=File:Bonus_marchers_05510_2004_001_a.gif *License:* Public Domain *Contributors:* Signal Corps Photographer ... 16
Figure 6 *Source:* https://en.wikipedia.org/w/index.php?title=File:Civilian_Conservation_Corps_-_NARA_-_195832.tif *License:* Public Domain *Contributors:* An Errant Knight, Djembayz, Hedwig in Washington, JMCC1, SBaker43 ... 17
Figure 7 *Source:* https://en.wikipedia.org/w/index.php?title=File:CampMurphy.jpg *License:* Public Domain *Contributors:* AnRo0002, File Upload Bot (Magnus Manske), Ianlopez1115, Morio, OgreBot 2, PeterWD, Sceadugenga, SecretName101, 1 anonymous edits ... 18
Figure 8 *Source:* https://en.wikipedia.org/w/index.php?title=File:26th_Cavalry_PI_Scouts_moving_into_Pozorrubio.jpg *License:* Public Domain *Contributors:* US military personnel ... 20
Figure 9 *Source:* https://en.wikipedia.org/w/index.php?title=File:MacArthur_and_Sutherland_s265357.jpg *License:* Public Domain *Contributors:* U.S. Army Signal Corps ... 21
Figure 10 *Source:* https://en.wikipedia.org/w/index.php?title=File:Douglas_MacArthur_MOH_Plaque,_USMA.JPG *License:* Public Domain *Contributors:* Ahodges7 ... 22
Figure 11 *Source:* https://en.wikipedia.org/w/index.php?title=File:Curtinmacarthur.jpg *License:* Public Domain *Contributors:* BotMultichill, Hawkeye7, Morio, Rcbutcher, Δ ... 25
Figure 12 *Source:* https://en.wikipedia.org/w/index.php?title=File:03_walker_macarthur.jpg *License:* Public Domain *Contributors:* C. Bottomley. The photo was sent to Peter Dunn by Douglas Walker, son of Brigadier General Kenneth Walker. It shows Gene ... 26
Figure 13 *Source:* https://en.wikipedia.org/w/index.php?title=File:FDR_conference_1944_HD-SN-99-02408.JPEG *License:* Public Domain *Contributors:* US Navy ... 28
Figure 14 *Source:* https://en.wikipedia.org/w/index.php?title=File:Douglas_MacArthur_lands_Leyte1.jpg *License:* Public Domain *Contributors:* U.S. Army Signal Corps officer Gaetano Faillace ... 31
Figure 15 *Source:* https://en.wikipedia.org/w/index.php?title=File:Leyte_beachhead.jpg *License:* Public Domain *Contributors:* US Army ... 32
Figure 16 *Source:* https://en.wikipedia.org/w/index.php?title=File:MacArthur,_Kenney_and_Sutherland.jpg *License:* Public Domain *Contributors:* Benchill, File Upload Bot (Magnus Manske), Hohum, Morio, OgreBot 2, Svensson1 ... 33
Figure 17 *Source:* https://en.wikipedia.org/w/index.php?title=File:Douglas_MacArthur_signs_formal_surrender.jpg *License:* Public Domain *Contributors:* United States Navy ... 35
Figure 18 *Source:* https://en.wikipedia.org/w/index.php?title=File:Macarthur_hirohito.jpg *License:* Public Domain *Contributors:* Bellerophon5685, BrokenSegue, Catsmeat, Docu, Esemono, Hawkeye7, Hohum, Infrogmation, Makthorpe, Materialscientist, Morio, Shika ryouse shomei, あばきー ... 36
Figure 19 *Source:* https://en.wikipedia.org/w/index.php?title=File:IMTFE_defendants.jpg *License:* Public Domain *Contributors:* Aschroet, Bohème, Bruno413, Kl833x9∼commonswiki, MChew, Morio, Takabeg, Takezawa takuma, WTCA, 庚寅五月 , 白拍子花子 ... 39
Figure 20 *Source:* https://en.wikipedia.org/w/index.php?title=File:IncheonLandingMcArthur.jpg *License:* Public Domain *Contributors:* Nutter (Army) ... 42
Figure 21 *Source:* https://en.wikipedia.org/w/index.php?title=File:Douglas_MacArthur_and_family,_1950.jpg *License:* Public Domain *Contributors:* File created by Tony Ahn. Original photographer unknown ... 45
Figure 22 *Source:* https://en.wikipedia.org/w/index.php?title=File:MacArthur_parade_in_Chicago_April_26,1951.jpg *Contributors:* User:Aprad 47
Figure 23 *Source:* https://en.wikipedia.org/w/index.php?title=File:Douglas_MacArthur_speaking_at_Soldier_Field_HD-SN-99-03036.JPEG *License:* Public Domain *Contributors:* Ardfern, BrokenSphere, Hawkeye7, Morio, SecretName101, 1 anonymous edits ... 48
Figure 24 *Source:* https://en.wikipedia.org/w/index.php?title=File:Macarthurmemorial.JPG *License:* Public Domain *Contributors:* Aschroet, BotMultichill, Hawkeye7, Jameslwoodward, Joebengo, Zolo ... 49
Figure 25 *Source:* https://en.wikipedia.org/w/index.php?title=File:Macarthurtomb.JPG *License:* Public domain *Contributors:* 24fan24∼commonswiki, Jllm06, Joebengo, OgreBot 2 ... 51
Figure 26 *Source:* https://en.wikipedia.org/w/index.php?title=File:General_Douglas_MacArthur_6c_1971_issue_U.S._stamp.jpg *License:* Public Domain *Contributors:* MrFrosty2, Robert Weemeyer ... 52
Figure 27 *Source:* https://en.wikipedia.org/w/index.php?title=File:West_entrance_of_General_Douglas_MacArthur_Tunnel,_San_Francisco,_California,_December_31st,_2014.jpg *License:* Creative Commons Attribution 3.0 *Contributors:* Mattpopovich ... 54
Image *Source:* https://en.wikipedia.org/w/index.php?title=File:US-OF1A.svg *Contributors:* - ... 69
Image *Source:* https://en.wikipedia.org/w/index.php?title=File:US-O3_insignia.svg *License:* Public Domain *Contributors:* Ipankonin ... 69
Image *Source:* https://en.wikipedia.org/w/index.php?title=File:US-O4_insignia.svg *License:* Public Domain *Contributors:* Ipankonin ... 69
Image *Source:* https://en.wikipedia.org/w/index.php?title=File:US-O6_insignia.svg *License:* Public Domain *Contributors:* U.S. Defense Logistics Agency ... 69
Image *Source:* https://en.wikipedia.org/w/index.php?title=File:US-O7_insignia.svg *License:* Public Domain *Contributors:* Ipankonin ... 69
Image *Source:* https://en.wikipedia.org/w/index.php?title=File:US-O8_insignia.svg *License:* Public Domain *Contributors:* Ipankonin ... 69
Image *Source:* https://en.wikipedia.org/w/index.php?title=File:US-O10_insignia.svg *License:* Public Domain *Contributors:* Ipankonin ... 69
Image *Source:* https://en.wikipedia.org/w/index.php?title=File:US-O9_insignia.svg *License:* Public Domain *Contributors:* Ipankonin ... 69
Image *Source:* https://en.wikipedia.org/w/index.php?title=File:Combat_Infantry_Badge.svg *License:* Public Domain *Contributors:* Ipankonin . 70
Image *Source:* https://en.wikipedia.org/w/index.php?title=File:US_Army_Master_Aviator_Badge.png *License:* Public Domain *Contributors:* CORNELIUSSEON, Darz Mol∼commonswiki, EricSerge, FieldMarine ... 70
Image *Source:* https://en.wikipedia.org/w/index.php?title=File:United_States_Army_Staff_Identification_Badge.png *License:* Public Domain *Contributors:* Illegitimate Barrister ... 70
Image *Source:* https://en.wikipedia.org/w/index.php?title=File:ExpertBadgeRP.jpg *License:* Public Domain *Contributors:* –Shotgun ... 70
Image *Source:* https://en.wikipedia.org/w/index.php?title=File:ArmyOSB.svg *License:* Public Domain *Contributors:* Manually converted to svg by User:Houdinipeter ... 70
Image *Source:* https://en.wikipedia.org/w/index.php?title=File:Medal_of_Honor_ribbon.svg *Contributors:* Ipankonin ... 71
Image *Source:* https://en.wikipedia.org/w/index.php?title=File:Navy_Distinguished_Service_ribbon.svg *Contributors:* - ... 71
Image *Source:* https://en.wikipedia.org/w/index.php?title=File:Distinguished_Flying_Cross_ribbon.svg *Contributors:* Ipankonin ... 71

Image *Source:* https://en.wikipedia.org/w/index.php?title=File:Air_Medal_ribbon.svg *Contributors:* Ipankonin ... 71

Image *Source:* https://en.wikipedia.org/w/index.php?title=File:Philippine_Campaign_Medal_ribbon.svg *License:* Public Domain *Contributors:* US Army ... 71

Image *Source:* https://en.wikipedia.org/w/index.php?title=File:Mexican_Service_Medal_ribbon.svg *Contributors:* Ipankonin ... 71

Image *Source:* https://en.wikipedia.org/w/index.php?title=File:Army_of_Occupation_of_Germany_ribbon.svg *Contributors:* Ipankonin ... 71

Image *Source:* https://en.wikipedia.org/w/index.php?title=File:World_War_II_Victory_Medal_ribbon.svg *Contributors:* Ipankonin ... 71

Image *Source:* https://en.wikipedia.org/w/index.php?title=File:Army_of_Occupation_ribbon.svg *Contributors:* Ipankonin ... 71

Image *Source:* https://en.wikipedia.org/w/index.php?title=File:Order_of_the_Bath_(ribbon).svg *Contributors:* - ... 71

Image *Source:* https://en.wikipedia.org/w/index.php?title=File:Legion_Honneur_GC_ribbon.svg *License:* Creative Commons Attribution-ShareAlike 3.0 Unported *Contributors:* Orem (wiki-pl: Orem, commons: Orem) ... 71

Image *Source:* https://en.wikipedia.org/w/index.php?title=File:BEL_Kroonorde_Grootkruis_BAR.svg *License:* Public Domain *Contributors:* Mboro ... 71

Image *Source:* https://en.wikipedia.org/w/index.php?title=File:PHL_Legion_of_Honor_-_Chief_Commander_BAR.png *License:* Public Domain *Contributors:* Wiki Romi ... 71

Image *Source:* https://en.wikipedia.org/w/index.php?title=File:Cavaliere_di_Gran_Croce_OCI_Kingdom_BAR.svg *License:* Public Domain *Contributors:* F l a n k e r ... 71

Image *Source:* https://en.wikipedia.org/w/index.php?title=File:TCH_CS_Vojensky_Rad_Bileho_Lva_1st_(1945)_BAR.svg *License:* Public Domain *Contributors:* Mboro Legion Honneur GC ribbon.svg by Orem Grande ufficiale OSSI medal BAR.svg by F l a n k e r Blason Boheme.svg by ... 71

Image *Source:* https://en.wikipedia.org/w/index.php?title=File:POL_Polonia_Restituta_Wielki_BAR.svg *License:* Creative Commons Attribution-ShareAlike 3.0 Unported *Contributors:* User:Orem ... 71

Image *Source:* https://en.wikipedia.org/w/index.php?title=File:NLD_Order_of_Orange-Nassau_-_Knight_Grand_Cross_BAR.png *License:* Public Domain *Contributors:* Wiki Romi ... 71

Image *Source:* https://en.wikipedia.org/w/index.php?title=File:SRB-SHS-YUG_Orden_Belog_Orla_sa_macevima_VKrst_BAR.svg *License:* Public Domain *Contributors:* User:Mboro ... 71

Image *Source:* https://en.wikipedia.org/w/index.php?title=File:JPN_Kyokujitsu-sho_Paulownia_BAR.svg *License:* Public Domain *Contributors:* Mboro derivative work:uaa ... 71

Image *Source:* https://en.wikipedia.org/w/index.php?title=File:Cavaliere_di_gran_Croce_BAR.svg *License:* Public Domain *Contributors:* F l a n k e r ... 71

Image *Source:* https://en.wikipedia.org/w/index.php?title=File:Order_of_Precious_Tripod_with_Special_Grand_Cordon_ribbon.png *License:* Public Domain *Contributors:* Миборовский ... 71

Image *Source:* https://en.wikipedia.org/w/index.php?title=File:HUN_Order_of_Merit_of_the_Hungarian_Rep_(military)_1class_BAR.svg *License:* Public Domain *Contributors:* User:Mboro ... 71

Image *Source:* https://en.wikipedia.org/w/index.php?title=File:Romanian_Order_of_Merit_Medal_Ribbon.png *License:* Creative Commons Attribution-Sharealike 3.0 *Contributors:* Dandvsp (talk) ... 71

Image *Source:* https://en.wikipedia.org/w/index.php?title=File:Taeguk_Cordon_Medal.png *License:* Creative Commons Attribution-Sharealike 3.0 *Contributors:* Dandvsp (talk) ... 71

Image *Source:* https://en.wikipedia.org/w/index.php?title=File:Order_of_Carlos_Manuel_de_Céspedes_-_Grand_Cross_(Cuba)_-_ribbon_bar_v._1926.png *License:* Creative Commons Zero *Contributors:* McOleo ... 71

Image *Source:* https://en.wikipedia.org/w/index.php?title=File:Order_of_Abdón_Calderón_1st_Class_(Ecuador)_-_ribbon_bar.png *License:* Creative Commons Attribution 3.0 *Contributors:* McOleo ... 71

Image *Source:* https://en.wikipedia.org/w/index.php?title=File:USA_-_DOS_Distinguished_Service_Award.png *Contributors:* Apocheir, Elisfkc, FastilyClone, OgreBot 2, Reguyla ... 71

Image *Source:* https://en.wikipedia.org/w/index.php?title=File:Croix_de_Guerre_1939-1945_ribbon.svg *License:* Creative Commons Attribution 3.0 *Contributors:* Boroduntalk ... 71

Image *Source:* https://en.wikipedia.org/w/index.php?title=File:UK_MID_1920-94.svg *License:* Public Domain *Contributors:* Mboro ... 71

Image *Source:* https://en.wikipedia.org/w/index.php?title=File:BEL_Croix_de_Guerre_WW1_ribbon.svg *License:* Public Domain *Contributors:* Croix_de_Guerre_1914-1918_ribbon.svg: Borodun derivative work: Mboro (talk) ... 71

Image *Source:* https://en.wikipedia.org/w/index.php?title=File:Philippine_Medal_of_Valor_ribbon.jpg *License:* Creative Commons Attribution-Sharealike 3.0 *Contributors:* EHDI5YS (talk) ... 71

Image *Source:* https://en.wikipedia.org/w/index.php?title=File:Distinguished_Conduct_Star_Ribbon_Bar.png *License:* Creative Commons Attribution-Sharealike 3.0 *Contributors:* Dandvsp (talk) ... 71

Image *Source:* https://en.wikipedia.org/w/index.php?title=File:Croce_di_guerra_al_merito_BAR.svg *License:* Public Domain *Contributors:* F l a n k e r ... 71

Image *Source:* https://en.wikipedia.org/w/index.php?title=File:Virtuti_Militari_Ribbon.png *Contributors:* User:Halibutt ... 71

Image *Source:* https://en.wikipedia.org/w/index.php?title=File:Greek_War_Cross_1940_3rd_class_ribbon.png *License:* Creative Commons Attribution-Sharealike 3.0 *Contributors:* Cplakidas ... 71

Image *Source:* https://en.wikipedia.org/w/index.php?title=File:MEX_Condecoracion_al_Merito_Militar_Primera_Clase.png *Contributors:* User:EricSerge ... 71

Image *Source:* https://en.wikipedia.org/w/index.php?title=File:Guatemalan_Armed_Forces_Cross.jpg *License:* Creative Commons Attribution-Sharealike 3.0 *Contributors:* EHDI5YS (talk) ... 71

Image *Source:* https://en.wikipedia.org/w/index.php?title=File:Philippines_Presidential_Unit_Citation.png *License:* Creative Commons Attribution-Sharealike 3.0 *Contributors:* User:EricSerge ... 71

Image *Source:* https://en.wikipedia.org/w/index.php?title=File:Korean_Presidential_Unit_Citation.png *License:* Creative Commons Attribution-Sharealike 3.0 *Contributors:* User:EricSerge ... 71

Image *Source:* https://en.wikipedia.org/w/index.php?title=File:PHL_Independence_Medal_ribbon.png *Contributors:* User:EricSerge ... 72

Image *Source:* https://en.wikipedia.org/w/index.php?title=File:United_Nations_Korea_Medal_ribbon.svg *Contributors:* - ... 72

Image *Source:* https://en.wikipedia.org/w/index.php?title=File:Ribbon_-_Pacific_Star.png *Contributors:* Col André Kritzinger ... 72

Image *Source:* https://en.wikipedia.org/w/index.php?title=File:Republic_of_Korea_War_Service_Medal_ribbon.svg *License:* Public Domain *Contributors:* Illegitimate Barrister ... 72

License

Creative Commons Attribution-Share Alike 3.0
//creativecommons.org/licenses/by-sa/3.0/

Index

www.ingramcontent.com/pod-product-compliance
Lightning Source LLC
Chambersburg PA
CBHW031538040426
42445CB00010B/590

* 9 7 8 9 3 5 2 9 7 9 4 5 5 *